Date Due

Ethel-			
Oct. 15			
Nov. 5			
Nov. 26			
ʻ18 ur '94			
July 21			
NOV 15 1994			

BRODART, INC.   Cat. No. 23 233   Printed in U.S.A.

HALFWAY TO THE GOLDFIELDS
A HISTORY OF LILLOOET

HALFWAY TO THE GOLDFIELDS
A HISTORY OF LILLOOET

Lorraine Harris

J.J. Douglas Ltd.
Vancouver

J.J. Douglas Ltd.
1875 Welch Street
North Vancouver, B.C.

Canadian Cataloguing in Publication Data

Harris, Lorraine, 1912-
   Halfway to the goldfields

   ISBN 0-88894-062-9

   1. Lillooet, B.C. - History. I. Title.
   FC3849.L54H37   971.1'4   C77-002050-X
   F1089.7.L54H37

Design and Book Production by Nancy Legue
Typesetting by Domino-Link
   Word and Data Processing Ltd.
Printed and bound in Canada

to my good friend **Renee Chipman,** without whose help and encouragement this book could not have been accomplished

and to my grandsons, **Scott and Michael:** great, great, great grandsons of Sergeant Major McMurphy of the Royal Engineers

My thanks go to **Mrs. Margaret Murray,** who
permitted me to search the files of the *Bridge
River-Lillooet News*, and to the many who became
my friends and willingly shared their family
stories:

Duffy Bryson
Mrs. Hilda Bryson
the late "Bob" Carson
Mr. and Mrs. Leo Cahill
Mrs. Barbara Harvey
Hilda Haylmore
the late Mrs. Maude Haylmore
Mrs. Richard Hoey
the late Tom Hurley
Mr. and Mrs. Bill Kane
the late Arthur Kwan
Tom Manson
Chief Sam Mitchell
Mrs. Myrtle Phillips
Len Russel
Hall and Fred Tingley
and my friend Jessie Leavans, who started it all.
Thanks also to Willard Ireland of the British
Columbia Provincial Archives.

For a source of confirmation to my research I am
indebted to F.W. Howay and E.O. Schofield's *The
History of British Columbia*

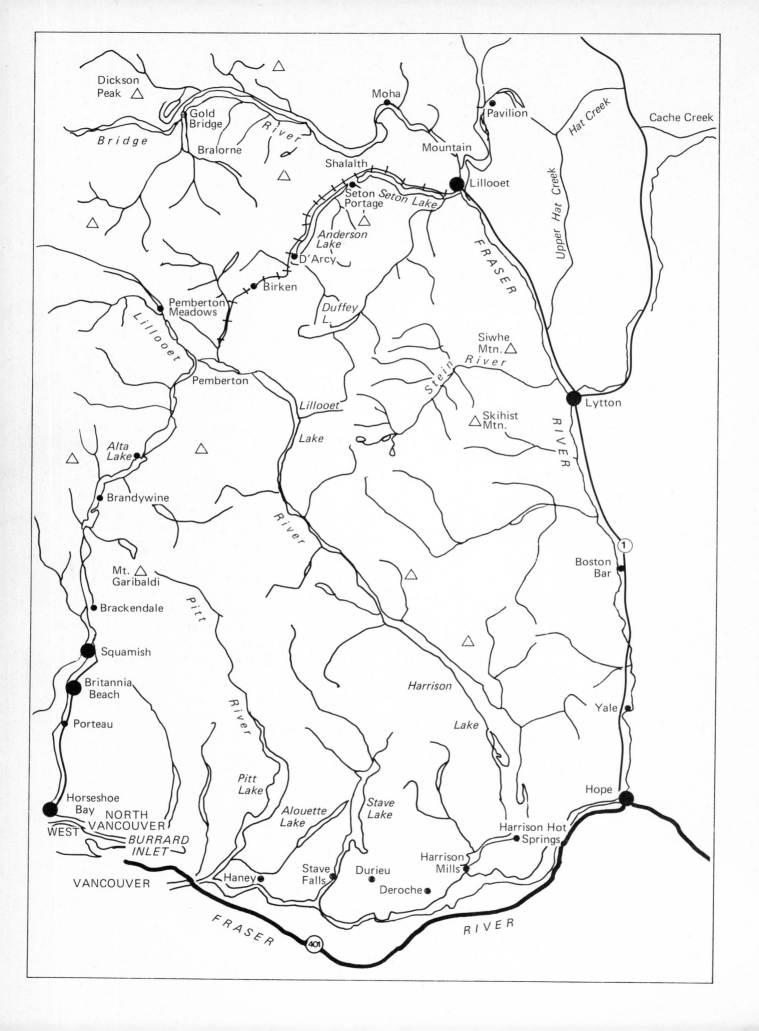

Foreword

This book has been written not only to preserve some of the early history of the Lillooet district but also to tell the stories of some of the pioneers who settled in the area. Being from a pioneer family, I have been dismayed that accounts of the area give no credit to the early settlers.

Little has been published in book form about our early settlers, so information has to be laboriously unearthed from old newspapers, microfilm, and clippings in libraries and archives.

Happily, I was able to collect the stories of the early families from their descendants, most of whom still live in the district; without their help this book would not have been possible.

It has been a most enjoyable experience meeting these friendly people and re-living the struggles of their parents and grandparents. I am deeply grateful to them for letting me tell their stories.

Lorraine Harris.

Introduction

Before British Columbia became a Colony most of its inhabitants were Indians hunting, fishing and trapping for food and clothing. They lived a simple life, taking from the land and

waters only what was necessary for their existence.

The British and Spanish explorers sailed the Pacific coast of North America and their discoveries spurred men to search for routes to the western ocean. Simon Fraser and David Thompson followed the rivers later named for them, and Alexander Mackenzie followed mountain valleys, rivers and trails to the coast.

There were many early explorers, but the forerunners of civilization in British Columbia were the Hudson's Bay Company men—traders, guides, and factors who built trading posts and developed trails between the few established areas. For guides and packers they hired Indians, many of whom settled in camps outside or near the forts. For the Indians, employment provided certain amenities, but it also brought alcohol, which has proved harmful to their way of life.

The discovery of gold in British Columbia in 1859 came about when an Indian showed a shiny stone to a Hudson's Bay Company trader who, recognizing its value, questioned him. The Indian said that he was squatting near a creek to take a drink when he saw the stone shining on the creek bottom, reflecting the sun's rays.

When the discovery became known, the ensuing gold rush with its hordes of men from all over the world created many problems. The territory became a Colony, and law officers and government officials were appointed. Roads, transportation, food and accommodation became of prime importance, and enterprising men and their families realized that not all the gold was in the goldfields; they could also earn money by supplying the needs of the miners.

Stopping places along the roads to the goldfields became necessary. Lillooet, situated about half way between the coast and the goldfields, quickly grew in importance.

Lillooet was born in 1858 on the banks of the Fraser, tucked into the foot of a mountain on a bench above the river. The Indians named it for the meeting of three waters—the Fraser River, Cayoosh Creek, and Bridge River. As the hub of traffic from the coast to the gold mines, and as one of the Colony's most important towns, it seemed destined to become a very large city.

The Royal Engineers built much of the road north to Alexandria and by 1860 Lillooet had blossomed into a supply centre for miners, packers, farmers and ranchers and the seat of government for the gold traffic.

Freight teams passing through Lillooet in the early 1900s

As the town grew, more and more miners wintered there instead of travelling the weary miles to the coast. It is said that ten thousand people once spent the winter in Lillooet and on the adjoining banks of the Fraser.

The town prospered, and pioneer names such as Manson, Martley, Hurley, Carson, Kane, Watkinson, Phair, Hoey and Bryson became well known up and down the Cariboo Wagon Road. Families began to settle in Lillooet, and churches, schools and the enforcement of law and order became essential. The government sent a magistrate and gold commissioner, the Anglican Church of Saint Mary the Virgin was built in 1861, and in 1873 a school was established. Doctors came and went and ministers and priests travelled regularly to Lillooet. The famed Judge Matthew Baillie Begbie travelled the Lillooet circuit and held court here, for as well as the adventurers stopping over in the town there were murderers, gamblers and claim-jumpers to be reckoned with. In the very early days there was not even a jail; the accused roamed freely in the streets.

Ranchers and farmers found ready markets in the mining camps. Cattle, hogs, chickens, and turkeys were raised to be sent north to the miners. Feed was grown in the perfect climate on the bench along the Fraser. Seed from Mexico was the beginning of highly sought-after alfalfa hay which grows profusely in this climate. The main crops of the farmers were turnips, potatoes and beans, including the now well-known Lillooet bean.

The town required flour mills, sawmills and brickyards, and in them English, Irish, Scots, Chinese, Indians, Americans and Australians worked side by side.

Lillooet's geographical setting is well described in the Annual Mining Report of 1889:

> The town of Lillooet is situated upon the plateau of the Fraser River, snugly lying under the lea of high, abrupt mountains, reminding one of the town of Helena, with the mighty Fraser rolling past, instead of a national highway. Mr. Allen, MPP, was quite enthusiastic over the merits of the little town under the hills and shewed us some splendid fruites and vegetables that were raised under the genial influence of their beautiful climate and irrigation. It is indeed a charming location and all that it requires is commercial life and enterprise, which will, no doubt, come in due time through the development of the mineral wealth of the surrounding country.

But when the wagon road was built through the Fraser Canyon, the main traffic bypassed Lillooet and its importance as a stopping place waned.

The town fortunes have fluctuated almost directly with mining on the banks of the Fraser and Bridge rivers and in the Bralorne area and with the good and hard times of the logging industry, but the old families stayed, optimistic that Lillooet had a good future.

CHAPTER
1

Those Who Came:
The Way They Travelled

British Columbia's First Highway

Lillooet, B.C.

Until the discovery of gold, little was known to the outside world of what is now the Province of British Columbia. It was then the Territory of New Caledonia, populated by Hudson's Bay Company men scattered in posts throughout the country for the purpose of trading with the Indians for furs.

On 8 July 1858, Sir Edward Bulwer Lytton introduced a bill into the English House of Commons setting out the boundaries of the Colony. The bill was passed on August 2 of that year, and the boundaries were defined as "The Rocky Mountains on the east, the Finlay branch of the Peace River and the Naas River (therein called Simpson's River) on the north, and the Pacific Ocean on the west, including the Queen Charlotte Islands and all the other Pacific Islands along the coast except Vancouver island," Vancouver Island

being a colony unto itself. Lytton suggested "the necessity of some organized government being established amidst a motley inundation of immigrant diggers, of whose antecedents we are wholly ignorant, and of whom perhaps few, if any have any intention of becoming resident colonists and British subjects." Judge Howay's history states, "Sir E.B. Lytton pointed out for this reason it was impossible to establish self-government, and that it was desirable that until some stable population existed the governor should be the law-maker, but with power to establish responsible government should the necessary elements appear." Thus James Douglas, Chief Factor of the Hudson's Bay Company and Governor of Vancouver Island, was able to make decisions for the Colony as the Queen's representative, without referring to the home government.

The gold that had been discovered on the banks and bars of the Fraser River brought thousands of men thrusting their way north by river and trail. Soon traffic was moving both north

The first section of B.C.'s first highway was built at practically no expense to the government, by the miners themselves working with the Royal Engineers who were brought out from England. Governor Douglas described the beginning of the road:

We have commenced the work of improving internal communications of the country as referred to in my despatch, July 1858, and have a party of 500 men now engaged in opening a road into upper Fraser's River by the valley of Harrison's River. A sternwheel steam vessel (the Col. Moody) is now running to the upper extremity of Harrison's Lake from where we have been cutting a road through the forest on the left bank of Harrison's River and Lillooet Lake to connect Anderson's Lake with Harrison's Lake the total distance between those two points, being about 80 miles of land carriage over a generally level country. The men employed in that important enterprise are gold miners, composed of many nations, British subjects, Americans, French, Germans, Danes, Africans and Chinese who *volunteered* their services immediately on our wish to open a practicable route into the interior of the Fraser River District being made public. They, moreover, proffered their services on terms so peculiar in themselves, and so advantageous for the country, that it would have been unwise of me to decline them. Each man, for example, on being enrolled into the corps paid into our hands the sum of $25.00 as security for good conduct. They receive no remuneration in the form of pay; the government having merely to supply them with food while employed on the road, and to transport them free of expense to the commencement of the road on Harrison Lake where the money deposit of $25.00 is to be repaid in provisions at Victoria prices, when the road is finished. The cost of the work will therefore not be heavy, nor exceed our means of repayment out of the revenues of the Gold District.

The organization of the corps is simple, yet effective, it being divided into 20 companies of 25 men, and each company under the command of the corps, a captain, who carries all the orders into effect, reports to the Commander of the corps, and draws upon the Commissary for the weekly supplies of food. An Engineer, with guides and Indians acquainted with the country, blazes the trees, and marks out the road, in advance of the main body. That route (north from Chilcotin) will be of the greatest advantage to the country, and when opened, will form the commercial highway into the interior of the districts, there being little probability of the existence of any other practicable route from the coast.

The Royal Engineers, sappers and miners were raised in England and were chosen for their special skills or trades. Their function was to assist the settlers of the new colony by dividing the land into parcels for sale or grants, and establishing a meteorological office, post office and land registry office.

and south as some brought out their gold and others gave up their search for the yellow nuggets.

Governor Douglas became alarmed at the influx of California miners and wrote to Sir E.B. Lytton, Colonial Secretary in England, asking that troops be sent post haste "to keep the peace and open up the country." The miners were a rough and ready lot, and, according to Douglas, represented "with some exceptions, a specimen of the worst of the population of San Francisco, the very dregs of society." He suggested in his request for help that "the affairs of government might be carried out more smoothly with even a single company of infantry."

Governor Douglas was the first to realize the need for an access road to the goldfields. In a dispatch dated 6 July 1858 to the Right Honourable Lord Stanley in England, he said that the miners needed some means of getting their gold safely to the coast and proposed a government escort service.

A route to the interior goldfields was of primary importance, and Lieut. R.C. Mayne of the Royal Navy, attached to the Royal Engineers during their stay in British Columbia, made a reconnaissance trip to investigate a possible route suggested by A.C. Anderson, the HBC Factor stationed on what is now Anderson Lake. Factor Donald McLean suggested that it would be polite to ask an old Indian chief, Captain St. Paul Lolo, to accompany them. He was crippled with a knee ailment and they were surprised at his agreeing to come, although as it transpired, without him they would have had many difficulties.

He guided them down the Thompson River to Riviere a la Cache (Cache Creek), through Riviere Au Chapeau (Hat Creek), and through the Marble Canyon to Pavilon (Pavilion). They followed the horse trail down the mountain on the east bank of the Fraser to Lillooet, then known as Cayoosh, where Lieutenant Mayne declared, "It is the prettiest spot I have seen."

In describing the trip, Mayne wrote in his book *Four Years in British Columbia and Vancouver Island* that they ate at "restaurants" —simple huts where a meal of bacon, beans, bread, salt, butter, tea or coffee could be had for a dollar, and where one could "select the softest plank in the floor to sleep on." There was little coin in use and change was weighed off in gold dust, which everyone carried in chamois-leather bags.

Lieutenant Mayne found that the food along the trail consisted almost exclusively of bacon and dampers with tea and coffee. He wrote: "The occasional grouse added to this but only if the bird was foolish enough to be on the route as when you are travelling with an object, time cannot be given to going out of the way to hunt up game."

Dampers were made from flour, baking powder or baking soda and enough water to make a heavy dough. They were rolled out to the size of a plate one or two inches thick, and then either fried in a pan with the bacon grease, or placed on a lightly greased pan and baked in the wood ashes of the fire. Healthy appetites are not particular, as Mayne noted: "Breakfast was ready and our appetites being freshened with a six hour walk, dampers of the consistency of saddle leather disappeared as if they had been puff paste."

Mayne travelled by steamer down Seton Lake to Seton Portage, a short portage between Anderson and Seton lakes. Two towns had been established at the portage—Wapping on the Anderson Lake side and Flushing on the Seton Lake side. A small gauge railroad connected the lakes. The wooden cars resembled open ore cars, but were more than adequate for transporting freight. Such heavy articles as the engine and accoutrements for the ferry being built at Alexandria were moved over this narrow gauge railroad to connect with the steamer at Flushing and on to the end of Seton Lake, whence they were transported over the wagon road to Alexandria.

After the trip down Seton and Anderson lakes, the reconnaissance group reached a flat meadowland called Birkenhead Portage or simply "the long portage." Here they enhanced their meals with wild peas, vetches, lettuce, and various berries. Through this stretch of land the Birkenhead River flowed. Captain Anderson had named the area in remembrance of his cousin who had been lost at sea on the S.S. *Birkenhead*. This portage was later called Mosquito Portage for obvious reasons, and was an easy route to Lillooet Lake.

The party travelled down Lillooet Lake via steamer, and then portaged to Port Douglas at the head of Harrison Lake. Lieutenant Mayne continued to Victoria and recommended to Governor Douglas that this be the route to the interior. The Canyon route, Yale to Lytton, was impassable at this time.

Lieutenant Mayne put Sergeant John McMurphy of the Royal Engineers in charge of road building and early in the fall of 1860 McMurphy and his detail travelled up Harrison Lake to Port Douglas. Here, according to McMurphy's diary, they "built 10 miles of road from Douglas to Mud Lake." When winter closed in, the men returned to Fort Langley.

Early view of Port Douglas on Harrison Lake

Provincial Archives, Victoria

At this time Port Douglas was a booming town of 2,000, teeming with Indians and miners, packers and wagons waiting to make the trip to the goldfields. In 1861 it had a wagon factory

The last of Frank Laumeister's camels for the Cariboo Road, 1888

operating at full production, and a sawmill and planing machine producing dressed lumber. In the surrounding area men were mining for gold, silver and quartz. St. Agnes Well (not to be confused with St. Alice Well, Harrison Hot Springs), ten miles from Port Douglas, became a stopover for the packers, and the hot springs afforded baths for the footsore, weary travellers. Beds and meals were also available.

In 1862 Frank Laumeister introduced camels as pack animals on this route, and the Lillooet trail became known as "the route of camels." He brought the animals up from California convinced that they would provide a cheap, effective means of transportation, being hard workers and needing less food than horses and mules do. However, the terrain proved too hard on the animals' feet and the rain made them sick. The camels had such an offensive odour that other pack animals would not work on the same trains or even pass a camel train on the road. Horses and mules would go over the banks and cliffs if forced into close proximity with the camels, and the packers would sue Laumeister for the loss of their animals. So the experiment failed, and the camels were turned out to graze on

the plateaus of the Thompson. For years they were a source of terror to horses and mules in the area, the last survivor dying about 1905.

The road and the steamers on the lakes brought civilization to Lillooet. Traffic came from Lytton in the south via horseback and riverboat; from the east through the Marble Canyon, Pavilion Lake and down to the banks of the Fraser; from the north it came from Clinton over Pavilion Mountain, and from the west it came up the lakes route. Lillooet was the hub.

On 23 June 1859, a journalist writing in the *British Colonist* gave a first-hand report on conditions in Lillooet:

> This place has been completely run out of everything eatable by the number of men coming down for stores. If I had been a trader and brought with me 20,000 pounds of bacon and 20,000 pounds of flour I could have got rid of the bacon before breakfast and had an empty house by dinner time. Some men have been here for a fortnight and not been able to get their supplies yet. People say this is going to be a great supplying point for the whole upper country. I hope so for it is far the prettiest and most eligible spot for a town that I have seen in the colony.

In 1860 the population of Lillooet was reported to be between four and five thousand people.

Sgt. Major
John McMurphy

Sergeant John McMurphy of the Royal Engineers

On 2 June 1862, Sgt. Major John McMurphy came with his men to Lillooet to work on the wagon road. They made camp across the river at Parsonville, named for Capt. Otis Parsons of the HBC.

Nearby, on the same side of the river, was the settlement of Marysville, named for the daughter of A.C. Elliott, a popular magistrate at Lillooet. The Hudson's Bay Company was building Fort Berens on this side also. Parsonville marked the start of the road and was designated Mile 0; all measurements were taken from this base. As Lillooet grew her importance overshadowed Parsonville, Marysville and Fort Berens, and they ceased to exist. Lillooet became Mile 0 and is so designated today.

Sgt. John McMurphy, with a background as soldier, miner and engineer, was well equipped to take on the duties of road building. He had served nineteen years in Her Majesty's forces before coming to the new colony and although entitled to the rank of Sergeant Major, he was often referred to as Sergeant John or "Jock" McMurphy. He had enlisted in Glasgow on 15 May 1840 and saw action in Africa and the Crimea, where he was commended for gallantry. On 23 September 1863, Sgt. Major "Jock" McMurphy was discharged from the Company of Royal Engineers in New Westminster.

In a letter to the Colonial Secretary, Mr. Good, he lists a statement of his services in B.C.:

I left New Westminster June 1859 with a detachment of Engineers for Douglas [Port Douglas], made a trail there to 10-Mile House; in the following year, 1860, went up again and made a wagon road from Douglas to the Little Lake, 29½ miles. In 1861 commenced work 7 miles from Hope and made a road from there to where the government trail goes into the Similkameen, all those roads were conducted by myself under orders of Capt., now Colonel Grant, RE in 1862 and 1863. May 26th, 1862 was resident engineer on the road from Lillooet to Alexandria, a distance of 198 miles and finished it with credit to myself and satisfaction to officers I served under.

In charge of the Lillooet road, he was responsible for approving the work done by the contractors who were building sections of road in remote areas. McMurphy was required to report to his superior officers regularly and to keep a record of all work done. He wrote in beautiful script a diary which is now in the Royal Engineers' museum at Camp Chilliwack.

June 3rd

Left Parsonville 10 AM and arrived ("24-Mile" ranch) Deep Creek—a distance of 14 miles. They started work at once.

June 6th

Fine weather. The work progressing steadily. One mule train passed into town (Lillooet) from William's Lake and one from Bonaparte River for provisions.

June 7th

A large train with provisions and Iron work for the steamer that is being built near Alexander a great many miners passed this way today also. There has been a good many miners returned today also who say the snow is too deep, and flour selling for 5s (five shillings) a pound.

June 9th

Train of 60 mules passed into town from The Dalles, Oregon, to purchase provisions.

June 10th

Train of ten beasts passed today from Salmon

Pavilion Mountain

River. Drivers state the Californians are leaving it for Cariboo, a great many miners have gone up today, principally Canadians. A case of Brandy and a box of preserves for our gruel arrived as we complained having nothing to eat but beans and bacon three times a day which is a very good thing now and then, but 21 times a week is too often.

June 22nd

Rode across the mountain [Pavilion] and had a look at every corner of it where it was possible to bring the road and decided that a good grade of 1 in 10 can be gotten with little trouble, at the same time condemned a bridge of 90 ft. that was nigh finished, as it had neither strength nor anything else about it that could recommend it.

There were 250 men working on Pavilion Mountain at this time. McMurphy and his assistant, Corporal Woodcock, did the actual "chaining" of the distance from Parsonville (Mile 0) and put up "mile-marks" indicating the distances. Along with the chaining, McMurphy made the final inspection of the road. If the contractors had done a good job, McMurphy gave them a certificate and with this they could collect from the government the agreed-upon price for construction. If the work was not finished to his satisfaction, he might issue a certificate with a guarantee in writing from the contractor that the road could be opened for traffic. At other times he withheld the certificate until the work was completed to his satisfaction.

The worst part of the whole road was the area down the north side of Pavilion Mountain, where a steep grade made zigzagging of the road and cribbing of the sides essential. The road today follows almost the exact route and is still difficult in poor weather. In the earlier days it was customary to drag a log behind a wagon to slow the vehicle so that it would not run over the animals. On the whole, however, the mountain road was considered very good.

July 17th

It is a first rate road both in grades and finish.

Everyone says the mountain is the best part of the road. There was 211 beasts passed this way today. There was 2 wagons arrived at our camp today one with 5-pair of oxen, drawing 2 tons. The other with 3 pair drawing 50-hundred weight and came out there they say quite easy.

July 19th

The road going well, a large train of 106 mules passed up this morning from Lytton, having come through Fountain Gap. Muleteers say packers from the other side (the Thompson R.) will all come this way when they hear of such a good road and such good feed for their cattle.

August 31st

Fine. Sunday. One of our workmen took ill Friday and died this morning and was buried this evening. I attended the funeral. He could not be kept longer as the smell of his body was strong.

In most places the road was eight feet wide, and the wonder of its being built over the high, steep Pavilion Mountain was next only to the wonder of the traffic the teamsters pushed over it. McMurphy's journal entry of 5 October 1862 reads,

"Sunday all men at work. 2 wagons came from Lillooet one with 8-yoke of oxen drawing 10,200 (lbs.), the other with 6-yoke drawing 7,000."

Evidence of the wealth carried over this road and through Lillooet is recorded on 8 October 1862:

"Snow fell last night. Threatening for more. 2 miners passed this AM with 12,000 dollars each from Williams Creek."

With these fortunes from "further up" passing by the road builders as they toiled for wages of fifty-four dollars a month, it was a wonder that Jock McMurphy was able to keep a full crew working. He had started with white labour but as goldfever attacked the men, many left for the goldfields. McMurphy then employed Indians and Chinese, who proved to be good and reliable workers.

On 8 August 1863, the road was completed from Parsonville to Alexandria. After the disbanding of the Royal Engineers in 1863, John McMurphy elected to stay in British Columbia, and built a house at 74 Mile House which he named Loch Lomond. After he had moved his family to Loch Lomond they operated a stage stop which the stage coach drivers noted as "a good place to stop, good food, good beds and everything taken care of." During 1864 and 1865 things went very well, until gold discoveries in other parts drew great numbers of men away from this route.

Government House, southern view, 1864.

Sergeant and Mrs. John McMurphy in 1859

In 1865 McMurphy received word from Dr. Tolmie of the HBC to come to Victoria, as his pension had arrived. He left for the coast, telling no one but his wife of his business there. He was gone fifteen days and returned to a tragedy. By his own account, "word got about that I had run away and when I returned to find my house a wreck, my horses, cows, pigs and poultry all gone, everything that was moveable, so I left with my family on Dec. 2nd and come down to New Westminster with hopes of getting employment from the Govt."

He was unable to find work, and with his family nearly starving he appealed unsuccessfully to Governor Seymour. Nor did help come from Colonial Secretary Good or other officials; McMurphy was forced to take jobs as a labourer to keep food on the table. He lived his life out in New Westminster with his wife and eleven children and died in 1906. He is buried in Fraser Cemetery, the resting place of many British Columbia pioneers.

Stagecoaching

While the engineers were pushing the road to Alexandria and a steamer was being built to continue the route to Quesnelmouth, the entrance to the goldfields, stagecoaches were being introduced in the more southerly regions. Freight wagons followed, bringing supplies in great quantities and taking less time than pack trains.

Stagecoaches became the only means of fast, relatively comfortable travel on the Cariboo Road, and their development contributed greatly to the life of Lillooet.

Bill Ballou's stage lines were the first in the Colony. He went to San Francisco at the beginning of the gold rush and made arrangements with Feeman and Company's Express to represent them in British Columbia. He established the first mail express, "Ballou's Pioneer Fraser River Express," in June 1858, charging fifty cents a letter from Victoria to Hope and two dollars from the Lower Fraser north. A few years later he started "Ballou's Cariboo Express," which operated to the Cariboo by way of the Douglas-Lillooet portage route, carrying the mail by stagecoach, horseback, canoe or on snowshoes—any way to get it through. When Ballou carried the mail on foot, the newspapers, the Victoria *Colonist* and *Chronicle*, sold for one dollar each copy. He carried the government mails gratuitously.

His service made headlines when in June 1862 the *British Columbian* of New Westminster noted, "Ballou and Co.'s Express arrived on Wednesday, making the trip from Williams Creek to Lillooet in five days and to this city in eight days. This express brought 447 letters and $18,000 in treasure."

In the fall of 1862 when Bill Ballou withdrew from the express business, the *British Columbian* said "he came to this country in 1850, since which time he has been instant, in and out of season, passing through hairbreadth escapes and innumerable hardships, in all of which Ballou never failed to connect." Bill Ballou is one of B.C.'s important pioneers.

On 2 March 1860, Captain William Jaffray formed a partnership with William H. Thain to "conduct a general express, to act as travelling agents and to do commission business between Victoria and British Columbia." On April 2 "Jaffray and Company's Express"—a steamboat express—began its regular service. The company maintained agents on the steamboats which ran from Victoria to New Westminster, and on the sternwheelers which plied the Fraser to Fort Hope and Fort Yale, and Harrison Lake to Port Douglas. From Port Douglas the company connected with Myer's Express, which travelled the Lillooet portage route regularly to the interior mines.

Jaffray's operated for one year and then sold out to Francis G. Barnard. The new company became known as "The BX Stage Lines" (Barnard's Express). In 1861 Barnard carried the mail up the difficult Fraser River route from Yale to Soda Creek, charging two dollars a letter—a price the miners willingly paid. Barnard is said to have started carrying the mail from Lillooet to north Cariboo for twenty-five cents a letter and saved enough money to buy one mule. The one-mule team grew to many teams and Barnard's Express became B.C.'s most famous freight line. In June 1862 the stages were going from Douglas as far as Pavilion, and by July 1863 they travelled to 154 Mile—Frank Wray's ranch. The fare from Port Douglas was fifty-four dollars.

Barnard was Ballou's most serious competitor, and in 1862 succeeded in taking over the mail contract.

A copy of the schedule of the British Columbia Express Compay advertises "650 miles of the best equipped stage lines in America." The schedule, which started at Ashcroft, provided thirty-six stops to Barkerville and offered semi-weekly service from May 15 to October 31 and a weekly winter and summer service from Ashcroft to Cache Creek, through the Marble Canyon to Pavilion and down to Lillooet. Weekly services were offered by the Alkali Lake, the Horsefly Line (150 Mile House to Horsefly), Quesnelle Forks Line (150 Mile House to Quesnelle Forks), and the Chilcotin Line (Soda Creek via Riske Creek to Alexis Creek).

Freighting on the Cariboo Road with the B.C. Express Company

Provincial Archives, Victoria

A coach and team of Barnard's Express on the Cariboo Road

Provincial Archives, Victoria

Steve Tingley: Stagecoach Driver

In 1864 Frank Barnard of the BX Stage Lines was establishing a regular express service on the Cariboo Road from Yale to Clinton to Soda Creek and on to Alexandria. He hired two young men to drive for him—Stephen Tingley and James Hamilton—and they became partners with him the same year. In 1871 the company was incorporated as the "B.C. Express Company." Barnard held half-interest and Steve Tingley and Jim Hamilton a quarter-interest each. When Hamilton died in Victoria, Barnard and Tingley acquired his interest.

The "B.C. Express" not only operated four and six horse-drawn stagecoaches but also owned steamers. In the late 1860s Barnard's "BX" bought out Deitz and Nelson, who ran an express business on the steamers between Victoria, New Westminster and Yale. In 1886, when Steve Tingley was sole owner of the "B.C. Express," he bought out Captain Wright's steamer line from Alexandria to Quesnelmouth and thus owned the express service from Victoria to Barkerville.

Tingley was born 13 September 1839, in Cumberland, N.B. He came to San Francisco in 1858. In 1861 he heard of the fabulous gold finds in B.C. and shipped out for Victoria. Once there he wasted no time in embarking on a steamer for Yale. The tall, slim, fresh-complexioned youth panned with the hundreds of miners at Yale, but was not very successful. Deciding it was time to move on, he took a hundred-pound pack on his back and walked the 400 miles to Barkerville. After two mediocre seasons of mining, he gave up and returned to Yale to open a harness shop. A short time later Frank Barnard hired him.

Steve Tingley was a young man who was said "to have the hands of a man accustomed to handling the ribbons." Because of his reputation as an excellent horse handler, Barnard chose him to go to Southern California to purchase the additional horses needed to keep up with the increasing business of the stage line. Tingley bought 500 horses, which he drove overland to Vernon, B.C. There the BX Company started the well-known BX Ranch.

Tingley was a good raconteur and enjoyed entertaining his passengers with tales of the early days of stagecoaching on the famous Cariboo

The young Stephen Tingley, stage driver

Road. One story he told with great pride was of driving Lord Dufferin on his trip to the Cariboo.

Lord Dufferin, Governor General of Canada, and Lady Dufferin made a state visit to B.C. in 1876, and on their itinerary was a trip to Williams Creek over the Cariboo Road. Because of his reputation as an expert driver, Steve Tingley was chosen to drive this important couple. For the occasion the famous Dufferin Coach was especially built in San Francisco for the BX Company. The Dufferin cost $1,200.00, a very high price in those days. It could be used as an open or closed coach and seated seven passengers, six inside and one beside the driver. Like the large stagecoaches operating in the southern U.S., the Dufferin had a "rack and boot" on the back for carrying the baggage. It was an elegant vehicle, and the horses were especially chosen for the trip, so the entourage attracted much attention along the route. James Hamilton drove another coach-and-four with the other members of the Governor General's party. So enjoyable was the trip to Lord Dufferin that he presented Stephen Tingley with a diamond pin as a memento. This was one of Tingley's most cherished possessions.

Passengers on the Cariboo Road

in the early 1860s Tingley, on a special mission for the law court, made a round trip of 380 miles in just thirty hours. Accompanied by Sergeant Major McMurphy and Sergeant Lindsay, he brought a murderer named Berry back to the gold diggings at Richfield to stand trial. Justice was swift then, and with the approval of the miners, Berry was hanged at once.

In January 1867 Steve Tingley was driving the express mail from Barkerville south. When the going became difficult, reported one of the passengers, "he got a large bobsled at 'the 150,' took the bed off a 6-horse coach that was there and secured it on the sleigh. This gave us some shelter from the weather which was below zero and with a little snow every day." He drove to Bluetent—127 Mile House—and spent the night, having admonished the passengers to be ready for an especially early start to try to make the forty-four miles to "the 83." They wakened to "20 inches of snow and no sign of the road." Tingley struck out anyway, the snow worsened, and he made the ten miles to "the 117" in five hours. There he "got a change of horses, a warming up and a good hot lunch, heated our rocks [a method travellers used to keep their feet warm under the rugs] and away we all went in good spirits, but at a slow walk with snow up to the horses' knees. We reached Bridge Creek, '100-mile' house, at dusk." The party stayed the night and when they awakened "it looked a desperate situation. It had snowed during the night, but Mr. Tingley was equal to the situation. He secured two horses from the proprietor and we started with three miles of hill to climb." The seven-mile trip to "the 93" took five hours. After warming up they started out again with "the snow . . . fully 5 inches in front of the sleigh bed. Finally we reached the '83' at 6 PM—17 miles in 13 hours with 6 good horses drawing us too."

The BX was the only company to travel the road in winter between Clinton and Barkerville, as all the others "laid in in the fall until June." Steve Tingley and the other BX drivers kept traffic lanes open, and the mail and express were much appreciated by all those who stayed north.

Shortly after a trip to California in 1868, Tingley returned to New Brunswick and brought back a bride to the west. The couple had two sons, Fred and Clarence. Mrs. Tingley was killed in an accident near Yale in 1873, and Stephen Tingley later married the daughter of Frank Laumeister, the man who introduced camels to British Columbia.

When Tingley became sole owner of the "B.C. Express," he moved the head office from Victoria to Ashcroft after the CPR had completed the railway to this point. He ran the BX until 1897, when he lost the mail contract to John Shields, Ryan Kilgour and Charles Miller of Toronto, and he sold out to them.

Stephen Tingley, who died in October 1915, was referred to in his obituary as "the pioneer whip of the Cariboo Road," a title of which he would have been proud.

Stephen Tingley

Cattle Drive on the Lillooet Trail

Cattle drive through Lillooet

The stagecoaches transported people and freight wagons carried supplies, but the best way to transport beef from the ranches in the Cariboo district to market was by long, arduous cattle drives. The Fraser Canyon route to the Lower Mainland was too precipitous for cattle driving, so the animals were driven north to Williams Lake or east to Kamloops, where unfortunately they brought lower prices than on the coast. Meanwhile the Lower Mainland residents were importing beef from the United States.

The Lillooet Trail was built to enable Cariboo beef to be driven to the coast. It was planned to connect with the Harrison-Lillooet road at D'Arcy, then to Pemberton, down the trail to Squamish, and over the mountains to Burrard Inlet. It was a wonderful dream which became a nightmare as successive promoters used the road to further their own gains, and thousands of dollars were wasted in the building and rebuilding of it.

The idea of a road from Lillooet to the coast was not new; it had been proposed as early as 1861 by Dr. Helmcken and pressed for by representatives from Lillooet to successive governments since 1869. Its importance is stated in the *British Colonist*, 28 June 1872:

It is the only apparently available avenue through which the stockraisers east of the Cascade Range may find an outlet for the produce of their industry, on the one hand, and through which, on the other hand, the communities on the seaboard might be supplied with domestic beef. The large stock-farming interests of the interior are paralyzed for want of such an outlet; and the large communities on the seaboard are, from the same cause, consuming foreign beef in payment of which the country is being drained of its wealth at the rate of something like $125,000.00 a year.

After four years of much agitation, political waffling and the expenditure of a great deal of money, the road was completed in October 1877, terminating at a point on Burrard Inlet between the Seymour and Lynn rivers.

Although construction was not finished until late in the season, almost too late for a cattle drive, Robert Carson, Richard Hoey and an Indian named Pecullah Kosta decided to drive a herd of 200 head to the coast market. They hoped to find sufficient feed along the route. The drive to the coast was not bad; the feed remained adequate and the trail was not too troublesome, except for the rough and steep portion above Cheakamus Canyon. However, from Squamish to near the mouth of the Seymour River, on Burrard Inlet, it became a nightmare. The terrain was rocky, winter rains made the trail a sea of mud, and some of the cattle nearly foundered. The cowboys had a difficult time keeping the herd moving over the swollen creeks and fallen trees. There was almost no feed for the weary animals, and by the time they reached the waters of Burrard Inlet they were in no condition to be sold for beef. But the herd was intact; not one animal had been lost. Carson and Hoey sold what they could of the herd and then were faced with wintering the rest on the mainland to fatten them for market in the spring. The cattle were taken across the inlet on scows and herded to the McLeery farm on the north arm of the Fraser, where Robert Carson spent the winter feeding and looking after them. Finally they were sold, and he headed back to his ranch on Pavilion Mountain. Their experiences led to an inquiry which concluded that the trail was not fit to drive cattle over.

Apart from being used by a few prospectors and mountaineers, the Burrard-Squamish trail fell into disuse and was finally abandoned to the mountain wilderness. The Squamish-Pemberton route remained a trail over which supplies were packed from the port of Squamish to the Pemberton Valley.

The Hoeys of Lillooet

The name Hoey appears often in early newspaper clippings, for Richard Hoey was active in Lillooet: co-owner of the first flour mill, and a partner with Robert Carson on the only cattle drive over the Lillooet Trail. Like many others, he believed that the trail would bring Lillooet into the limelight as a big city of the interior. He also hoped it would bring riches-on-the-hoof to the struggling ranchers who had to drive so far for smaller markets. Hoey was a strong advocate of the road, and was constantly frustrated by the unnecessary delays in building it. Forthright in his opinions and with the courage of his convictions, he was one to be counted on any issue which he considered important.

Richard Hoey and his brother Tom came from Ireland to join the forty-niners. After the California rush slowed down, they pushed north in 1858 to seek gold in B.C., but finally gave up the search and settled in Lillooet.

Tom owned land on Pavilion Mountain adjoining the Carsons and ranched there for some time, eventually selling out to Robert Carson.

Richard bought farmland on the flats and was granted forty acres on Texas Creek Road. He owned the first water rights on Lillooet Creek, very possibly the first water rights registered in B.C. He also had grazing land—two quarter sections—at Pavilion. He married the daughter of Augustus and Catherine Schubert, who had come from Fort Garry to Kamloops with the Overlanders. While at Kamloops Mrs. Schubert gave birth to a daughter, the first white girl born there. At Kamloops, the Overlanders split into two groups, and the Schuberts joined those who came down over Pavilion Mountain to Lillooet in 1862. The Richard Hoeys were later divorced.

Many stories have been told of Richard Hoey, but one in particular epitomizes his code of ethics. Once, when he was a stipendiary magistrate in Lillooet, he got quite drunk (not an unusual occurrence). So rigid was he in upholding the law that he came to court in the morning hung over, opened the books and fined himself five dollars for being drunk and disorderly.

Another of his characteristics was his Irish sense of humour. He had been well educated in Ireland and was able to bandy words with the best. One time he was in Clinton when his friend Judge Begbie was holding court and Richard was called for jury duty. He was not chosen to serve on the

The house built by Richard and Thomas Hoey in 1861, as it looked about 1900

jury, but later came into court "corned up and smoking a cigar." When Judge Begbie said, "No smoking in court, please," Hoey replied, "Your honour, this is not a five cent cigar, it is a twenty-five cent cigar." There was no answer from the bench. No doubt Judge Begbie thought better of engaging the cheerfully inebriated Richard in a debate, and so Hoey stayed on to watch the proceedings, smoking his cigar.

After his divorce, Richard lived alone on his farm and when he grew old, he sent home to Ireland for his nephew and namesake. Together they operated both the Texas Creek and town farms. Young Dick bought ninety acres where the Lillooet hospital now stands, and eventually married the daughter of Overlander Joseph L'Itallienne, an exceptionally honest, hard-working wheat farmer from Quebec. "French Joe," as he was known, came to Lillooet in 1862. In 1879 he went back to Quebec, married a schoolteacher, and returned with her to Lillooet in 1880. They lived at the 12 Mile ranch on the Pavilion road. Two daughters were born there, Louise Marie in 1881 (who was to marry young Dick Hoey), and Delina Clara (who would marry prospector Arthur Noel). By 1884 Mrs. L'Itallienne was so homesick that she could think of nothing except going back to Quebec. Part of her problem was that she spoke no English and so had difficulty conversing with the Lillooetans, few of whom spoke French.

Joe sold the ranch, and the family travelled by stagecoach from Lillooet to Yale, where Mrs. L'Itallienne got a berth on a riverboat. In 1884, the easiest, safest, and fastest way to get to Quebec was by a circuitous route, from Yale down the Fraser by boat to New Westminster, steamer to Victoria, thence to San Francisco and overland on the Union Pacific Railway to the Province of Quebec. The two L'Itallienne girls were nine months and twenty-six months old when they took this long trip. It is quite possible that theirs was the last ride on a Fraser sternwheeler.

Mrs. L'Itallienne was happy in French Canada and stayed there fourteen years. "French Joe" came back to Lillooet and built four houses. These he rented to support his family in the east. The children attended school in Quebec at the Convent Rivier d'Ulout. In addition to their academic lessons, they also learned to sew beautifully. This talent stood Louise and Delina in good stead later when they sewed and taught sewing for a living.

On 10 March 1898, Mrs. L'Itallienne and the girls came back to Lillooet to join Joe. They settled near the Fountain ranch and Joe worked for Dick Hoey at Texas Creek ranch. Eventually the L'Italliennes moved to the Texas Creek farm and soon after, young Dick Hoey married Louise Marie. Their first home was the log cabin that still stands on the Texas Creek farm. The young Hoeys lived at the farm until their uncle Richard died in Lillooet, and then they moved to the town farm, remaining there until the Texas Creek farm was sold. Two children, Violet and Richard John (Dick), were born in Lillooet.

The PGE stopping at Lillooet

The P.G.E. Railway

With the closing of the Lillooet Trail, Lillooet—being some fifty miles from Lytton and the Fraser Canyon route—was cut off from the mainstream of traffic. The town suffered from being bypassed, and it was not until 1915, when the first "Pacific Great Eastern" train from Squamish came through, that Lillooet was connected to the coast once more. The development of this railroad has been a some-time thing, but it has now come into its own as an important link between the coast and the interior of B.C.

The birth date of the PGE was 25 April 1907, when the "Howe Sound, Pemberton Valley and Northern Railway" was formed to operate a railroad from the mouth of the Squamish River to the Cheakamus River and on to Anderson Lake. It was to become a railroad of many names—from the "Howe Sound, Pemberton Valley & Northern" in 1907, to the "Howe Sound and Northern" in 1910, to the "Pacific Great Eastern" in 1912, to the "British Columbia Railway" in 1972.

The financial backer of the "Howe Sound and Northern" was the "Great Eastern Railroad" of England, and to honour this company the new railroad was named the "Pacific Great Eastern."

The first passenger trains were put on the line in 1915. To say this was an advantage would be a vast understatement—it was practically rebirth to the little settlement on the Fraser. Lillooet's importance had almost directly fluctuated according to the mining in the area. Now there was opportunity for agriculture to be an important part of the town's economy, with fast delivery to a large market. Ranching, too, could flourish with direct transportation of cattle to the city. It was hoped that people would flock back to make Lillooet once again one of B.C.'s more popular towns.

Lillooet became a central point for the railway; here extra engines were added to the trains for the climb over the mountain to Clinton. This created more jobs for the almost dormant town. Even mining companies renewed their interest with the advent of good transportation. Lillooet took on new life.

Myrtle and Alex Phillips of Alta Lake

There are those who still remember the building of the railroad; one couple who were a part of the early days of the PGE were Myrtle and Alex Phillips of Alta Lake.

Before the PGE had progressed beyond Brackendale, this young couple from Vancouver had heard of some wonderful fishing lakes near Squamish. They listened to a trapper named John Miller extol the beauties and great fishing of Alta Lake, and Alex, an ardent fisherman, had to see for himself. He and his wife, a great outdoors girl, boarded the Union steamship at Vancouver, travelled up Howe Sound to Squamish, and there found a stage which took them to Brackendale. The rest of the way was by "shank's mare." A long walk over a pack trail, steep in many spots, but with unbelievably beautiful scenery, brought them to Alta Lake, which was all that John Miller had said and more. They went back for three years in a row, from 1911 to 1913. By the third year Alex Phillips was so enamoured of the country and the excellent fishing that he was convinced a fishing lodge would be successful. They had little money, but with the help of a friend they managed to buy 100 acres on the lake.

In 1914 they moved permanently to the lake and Mrs. Phillips's father, a builder from Maine, came out to help them put up their first structure. With Myrtle and her father on the land, Alex Phillips continued working in Vancouver to keep them in bacon and beans while the building progressed.

Finally the log building was finished; it contained bedrooms for guest accommodation, a kitchen, store, post office, and living quarters. The couple's struggle for survival was far outweighed by their joy in the country and in owning their own piece of wilderness, which they named Rainbow Lodge.

The PGE built the roadbed and laid tracks as they went along. On 14 September 1914, building started from Cheekeye, and by the end of the year 58 miles of track had been laid. By the end of 1915, track was laid to Chasm, 176 miles north of Squamish. While construction was going on, the work crews were lodged in primitive camps at about 15-mile intervals. As they neared Rainbow Lodge the crews came to the lodge as often as possible for Myrtle Phillips's excellent meals. When the tracks had been laid as far as Rainbow, the engineer would give one howling blast of his whistle about one mile down the road, Mrs. Phillips would get up regardless of the hour, and by the time the train returned after turning at Mon's Wye she would have a breakfast ready of porridge, bacon, eggs, toast and lots of steaming coffee. She collected meal tickets from each crew member, redeeming them from the PGE for thirty-five cents a ticket.

By April 1915 the PGE wanted to run a special fisherman's train to Rainbow Lodge. Although Alex and Myrtle Phillips did not feel that they were ready to open, they agreed, and twenty-four guests arrived. The fishing was excellent despite the fact that the lake was just cleared of ice and this was not considered the most ideal time for fishing. Those who came had a successful weekend—they were fed, housed, and taken fishing for two dollars a day—and returned to the city a very happy group.

In the same year the PGE pushed on to Lillooet, and passenger cars were attached to the back of the work trains. There was no dining accommodation, so both east- and west-bound passengers were fed at Rainbow Lodge. When the railroad put the passenger cars on the road, a one-line telephone wire was strung along the tracks to be used solely for train communication. Telephones were attached to poles along the way, and people could phone into Squamish in an emergency. Mrs. Phillips would phone to find out how many passengers she was to feed, and would have delicious meals ready when the train stopped. She served meat or trout, vegetables from her garden, and desserts and hot biscuits that made her famous. Because of unpredictable conditions along the way, the train was not always on time and Mrs. Phillips had to be prepared for these delays. The train only stopped long enough for the passengers to consume the meal, and keeping the food ready to serve was not an easy feat in those days of wood stoves and no refrigeration.

The Phillipses' life was not easy, but this pioneering couple played a worthwhile part in the building of the railroad to the interior.

CHAPTER
2

Those Who Were There: The Indians

Chilcotin horsemen

Indians of the Area

The Indians of the Lillooet area were essentially peaceful, although their pride of race and pride of possession of their tribal hunting grounds at times brought them into conflict with each other. The neighbouring Chilcotins, from the Chilcotin Plateau country, were strong and proud of their ability to travel long distances at a hard pace and would stray far from their own territory in search of new hunting grounds. They travelled to the Bridge River through the Taseko country and even as far south as Yale.

One Chilcotin war party travelled through Big Creek (in the Chilcotin area), through Graveyard Valley, over Low Pass, down Tyax (Tyaughton)

Creek and across Spruce Lake, where they left their horses. Then they came on foot across Gun Creek, up the Gun Lakes to the Bridge River, and down this river to just above the present dam, where they made rafts and crossed over to the Hurley River. From there they went over the mountain and down the Lillooet River where they raided Pemberton. One look at the map shows what a long hazardous trip this was for the purpose of raiding.

Before the white man came seeking furs and then gold, the natives traded among themselves for what they needed. Then the Hudson's Bay Company established trading posts, and the Indians often gathered around these forts.

The Indians of the Lillooet area were people of many tribes, and each tribe had its own chief and village. They went north in summer and returned to their own land in the fall when the Fraser salmon ran. They especially liked to fish from the high rocks near the present Lillooet

Lillooet tribespeople, placer mining

The Indians were not indolent; as well as doing their own work, they were ready to accept employment from explorers, miners, and other travellers who wished to hire them as packers, trackers, guides and cowboys. They hunted for their food, tanned hides for moccasins and clothing, ate meat, and wasted little. The berries along the creeks and in the mountains were dried for winter use or were made into a kind of cake. They made cakes called whyelkine from lichens which grew on the pines. According to Lieutenant Mayne, they prepared these by removing the lichen from the twigs and bark, steeping it in water until it was quite soft, and then wrapping it well in grass and leaves to prevent it from burning while it cooked betwen hot stones. It was cooked ten to twelve hours, and when done was pressed into a cake.

The tribes at Pavilion and the Fountain lived in "keekwilly holes" in winter and teepees made of tanned hides and poles in summer; these they could fold up and carry with them. The keekwilly holes were deep trenches dug about ten feet long and eight to ten feet wide in which entire families lived. Over the holes the Indians laid large poles which they covered with sods or hides, leaving a hole so that the smoke from their fires could escape. This mountain region becomes cold in winter, and the keekwilly holes below ground level offered protection from the elements. When the whites arrived and built temporary houses of sod and more permanent log houses, the Indians copied their construction.

On the road to Pavilion there are still evidences of the rock bake ovens the Indians used. They were made in the shape of an igloo, with a hole at the top to let the smoke escape and another in the side at ground level, for draught.

Lieutenant Mayne of the Royal Engineers came through this way in 1858-59, and wrote of the Indians he met. He described how the Indians made their clothes from softly tanned deer hides and ornamented them with beads and porcupine quills. They also "copied the Spanish wooden saddle for riding and made bridles of simple cord or often the hair of the wild sheep for it cannot be called wool, plaited. The middle of this is passed through the horse's mouth and hitched around its lower jaw and the ends brought up on each side of his neck."

He wrote, "they spoke French not of the purest but they had a useful knowledge of French. It was the language spoken by the large number of Canadian Voyageurs who first came across the mountains in the service of the HBC and their trade at the inland posts is most carried on in French."

bridge and the banks of the Bridge River, which they called Hoyshen, south to below the confluence of the Fraser River and Cayoosh Creek. The racks for drying their fish were long in evidence along the banks of the Fraser.

Lieutenant Mayne hired Indians whenever he could, and he learned much about their ways. One of the first discoveries he made was that they loved military dress. The Royal Engineers only wore their uniforms on the most formal occasions, but Mayne found that even a service cap was sufficient to command the highest respect. "I wore an old uniform cap which I always found had a capital effect upon the Indians, inspiring them with an idea of the wearer's exalted position as 'Hyas Tyhee' or great chief. A HBC greatcoat—a sort of blue frock coat made with a hood and the gold lace on the cuffs—signifying the lieutenant's rank, added to the effect and which was worn before the natives upon all particularly important occasions." Mayne wrote,

> ...the majority of Indian parties have now adopted the dress of Europeans and turn out for the journey in trowsers and shirt, usually carrying an old coat of some sort, which they are careful to put on nearing a town. I have known them to be absurdly particular about this ceremony. I once journeyed with half a dozen Indians, each one of whom positively carried a suit of clothes in a bundle on his back for more than three weeks to have the satisfaction of wearing them at Port Douglas. When we were within a mile of the place the party halted, untied their bundles, donned their clothes and painting their faces bright red, filed into the town with dignified gravity. Shoes they would or could not adapt although they always insisted on being issued a pair, which they carried on their back packs, this was for effect to complete the costume. They travelled either barefoot or in moccasins —undecorated by beading or embroidery—in fact a plain piece of buckskin laced around their feet with thongs of the same skin sufficed for moccasins. I have seen occasions when an elk was killed by me, and within an hour after its death all the meat has been slung on their backs and its skin laced to their feet.

He noted that "while the Indians laugh and talk or busy themselves mending and patching their moccasins, turning and twisting them about in every direction to find a sound part to serve as a sole to protect the foot for the next day's journey over the rocky trails, a pipe was smoked." At night the Royal Engineers slept in tents and the Indians around a fire, and "no matter how cold the night, the Indian invariably strips to sleep and lies with his blanket about him, feet toward the fire. Even when camped in snow, I have observed they always take off their clothes."

The Indian objected to travelling without a companion from his own tribe, and so a traveller was compelled to hire two Indians. Indian guides and packers always expected a present before starting off, and, observed Mayne, it was a good idea to remember the wife, too, as a gift to her was more conducive to starting the man on his journey than anything else. The Indian wanted a "cultas potlatch," literally a useless present for which nothing was expected in return. Tobacco or a clay pipe was a good choice of gift. "Smoking the Indians learned from the whites and they learned by inhaling the great gulps, after a few minutes of which they were thoroughly intoxicated. They did not exhale and this caused the dizziness. This effect did not last long, about a quarter of an hour, but left them feeling very much worse than before smoking." They liked the feeling of light-headed abandon and it was not long until some became addicted and would work for a little money and tobacco.

Besides respecting a uniform, the Indians also admired a man who was a good shot, an employer who could bring down a bird on the wing or a deer running. A man who "could walk the Indians well of their legs" the first day of the journey gained their everlasting respect.

After mining on the Fraser near Lillooet became a lucrative source of income, Indians joined whites and Chinese in the search for gold. From 1890 to 1900 Indian families in trains of covered wagons travelled over Pavilion Mountain to work in the mines and pan for gold on the rivers. Many made good money at mining and were considered excellent workers.

The Lillooet tribe was part of the Interior Salish group along with the Shuswap, Thompson, and Okanagan tribes. The Lillooets, whose boundaries were the Seton, Anderson, Lillooet, and Harrison Lakes, adjoined the territory of the Coast Salish and were in frequent contact with the easy water routes. Like the Coast Salish, the Lillooets were fishermen. In late summer they fished with nets and spears from the river banks. In the fall and winter they trapped and hunted, often trading the hides. Their villages were not permanent, for the Lillooets followed the game and set up home wherever it was to be found.

Adding to their food supply of meat and fish, they gathered wild onion, wild carrot, bracken root and wild clover, which they dried and stored. They used the tender young shoots of flowering raspberries and salmonberries as greens which they boiled. With wild berries and nuts to add to the meat, fish, and vegetables, the Lillooets enjoyed a healthy diet.

They were excellent basketmakers, weaving baskets from grasses and split roots and using thin strips of bark or dyed grasses to create decorative patterns.

Their tools were made from igneous rock, bones, horn, and wood and their knives, arrowheads and spear points were of chert, jasper, quartz or obsidian. They used the harder nehrite for chisels and wedges, but for felling and splitting trees they used horn and wood tools.

Hunting bows were of yew or juniper wood and decorated with horsehair or bird scalps. The owner would paint his guardian spirit design on his bow. The bow string consisted of fine threads of sinew twisted together.

Their clothing consisted of shorts, breech clouts, hiplength leggings, robes, capes and moccasins. For warm winter clothes they used rabbit, bear and bird skins as well as tanned hides. For wet weather they wore short cloaks made from woven fibres of sagebrush, willow bark, and sometimes bullrushes. Some had winter cloaks made from beaver, lynx and bear hides. Moccasins were made of buckskin sewn with deer sinew, and winter socks were of soft furs, with the fur side worn in.

Indian Religion and Language

The Lillooets did not believe in a Supreme Being, or "the Old One," but they did believe in "the Chief," or "Chief of the Dead"—he who guarded the shades where the souls went and who would one day gather the bones and dust of the dead and make new bodies for souls to enter. They believed that the trail leading to the "land of the shades," which they thought was underground, was dry and dusty, and a huge rock wall separated the resting place of the souls.

When a Lillooet couple was close to having a child they were inhibited by taboos. The mother-to-be was not to look at anything ugly for fear of deforming the child she carried, and immediately before the birth the mother, with an elderly woman of her tribe, went into seclusion. Once the child was born and the father bathed, the taboos were removed. This ritual was not unlike that of the Coast Salish new fathers, who swam during the birth to cleanse the way into the world for their offspring.

The Lillooets divided the year into five seasons: spring, summer, early fall, deer hunting time and the rest of the year. Each season was divided into twelve moons with such names as "the hunting moon"; "going-in-time" for cold weather; "the bucks shed antlers and become lean"; "spring winds time," "coming forth time."

Good conduct and good character were important to the Lillooets and were impressed on their children from a young age. Boys were told often "it is bad to steal because people will laugh at you and impose upon you and the women will say that you should wear a skirt," and "it is bad to be quarrelsome because your friends will avoid you and your wife will not stay in your house."

The Lillooet Indians loved games and gambling. Men, women and children had their own games, and they entertained each other by wrestling matches, dart games, and competitions in marksmanship.

As the white population increased the churches sent missionaries into the field, and many Indians were converted to Christianity. The majority of the travelling priests and ministers were Catholic and many were French. One of these was a Father Le Jeune, who devised the first written language for the Indians. Each tribe had its own dialect, and as some tribes could not understand others, Chinook, a general trading language using European words, had been accepted by most. Many white men used Chinook, but priests and ministers had difficulty teaching catechism, prayers and hymns, for there was still no written Indian language. Father Le Jeune produced several polyglot manuals, including a catechism, in the Duployan shorthand which he had learned in France as a student. The catechism, published in Kamloops in 1896, was in English, Latin and Chinook.

Some Lillooet Indian people would ask their white friends to translate in formal situations when their English was inadequate. John Digby was often called to court by the presiding judge in New Westminster to translate for Indians.

The following is a brief "dictionary" of Chinook that was published in 1858 by Alexander C. Anderson in *Handbook and Map to the Gold Region of Fraser's and Thompson's River....*

Language used by the different Indian Tribes, French and Half-Breeds, of Frazer's River, Puget Sound, and surrounding country, as the means of Conversation with Americans.

Waw Waw ....To speak
Nika I
Mika ....You
Yaka ....He or She
Nesika ....We
Mesika ....We (plural)
Klaska ....They
Klacksta ....Who
Man ....Man
Klootchman ....Woman
Tenass klootchman .....Girl
Tenass man ....Boy
Mokoke house ....A store
Moola ....Saw mill
Kanim ....Canoe
Issick ....Paddle
Chuck ....Water
Sockally tyee .The Almighty
Kapo ....A relative
Chitch ....Grandmother

Boston ....American
Pesioux ....French
King George, Eng. Scotch, Irish.
Sitcum Siwashe ...Half-br'd
Tyee ....Chief
Elitee ....Slave
Ou ....Brother
Ats ....Sister
Oloman ....An old man
Lemeyi ......An old woman
Sun ....Day
Polakley ....Night
Tenass polakley .....Sunset
Sitcum sun ....Noon
Tenass sun ....Morning
Oke oke sun ....To-day
Tumalla ....To-morrow
Tamanass man ......Indian Doctor
Chickamen .....Metals of all kinds

Articles of Food and Clothing

Muck a muck ......anything good to eat

Pish ....Fish
Sabud ....Salmon
Tenass Sabud ....Trout
Mowitch ....Venison
Oleally ....Berries
Pire oleally ....Ripe berries
Cold oleally ....Cranberries
Pill oleally ....Strawberries
Wapito ....Potato
Molas ....Melasses
Shuga ....Sugar
Sil ....Cloth
Le Shawl ....Shawl
La wane ....Oats
Lum ....Rum
Pire chuck ....Ardent spirits
Skin shoes ....Moccasins
Chickamen shoes .....Horse shoes

Kloch kloch ....Oysters
La kootche ....Clams
Kleman sapalel ......Flour
Sapalel ....Wheat
Le Biscuit ......Hard bread
Stick shoes ....Shoes
Tootoosh ....Milk
Gleece ....Grass
Tootoosh Gleece .....Butter
Pasissee ....Blanket
Seapooloe ....Cap
Capeau ....Cook
Seekolicks ....Pants
Lalopa ....Ribbons
Akacpooit ....Needle
Sil sil ....Buttons
Klapite ....Thread
Kamoosack ....Beads
Luckwullah ....Nuts

Animals, Birds, Fish, etc.

Kuitan ....Horse
Moos moos ....Cow
La mutto ....Sheep
Kramox ....Dog
Pish pish ....Cat

Kusbaw ....Hog
Mowitch ....Deer
Itsoot ....Bear
Quitchaddy ....Rabbit
Swaawa ....Panther

Skudee ....Squirrel
Skubbyou ....Skunk
Man moos moos ....Ox
Korey kuitan .....Pace horse
Le lo ....Wolf
Le cock ....Rooster
Le pole ....Hen
Le sap ....Egg
Tenass la kootche ...Muscles
Tenass moos moos ......Calf

Moolack or moose ....Elk
La tate ....Head
La pea ....Foot
Tee owit ....Leg
Yachoot ....Belly
La pooshe ....Mouth
Leeda ....Teeth
Ena ....Beaver
Ninamox ....Otter
Olikhiyou ....Seal
Le mule or hyas Kolon .Mule
Kulla kulla ....Birds
Yakolla ....Eagle
Mauk ....Duck
Shakirk ....Hawk
Waugh waugh ....Owl
Smock mock ....Grouse
Skad ....Mole
Soolee ....Mouse
Oluck ....Snake
Quanice ....Whale
Quiceo ....Porpoise
Oyakut ....Trail or road
Quass ....Fear, afraid
Tzae ....Sweet
La table ....Table
Sockally ....High
Keekwully ....Low, beneath
Yoolkut ....Long

Siyah ....Distance
Tenass ....Small
Hyas ....Large
Skookum ....Strong
Wake Skookum ......Weak
Le lang ....Tongue
Seeah hoose ....Eyes
Sharty ....Sing
Solux ....Angry

Patle ....Full

32

Patlum . . . . .Drunk or full of rum
Lope . . . . .Rope
Initie . . . . .Over, across
Klip . . . . .Deep
Keemta . . . . .Behind
Hooey hooey . . . . .Exchange, barter
Kopa . . . . . . .From, towards
Olo . . . . . .Hungry or thirsty
Quis quis . . . . . . .A straw mat
Paper . . . . .Paper
Lapiage . . . . .A trap
Alloyma . . . . .Another
Miami . . . . . . .Down stream
Machlanny . . . . . .toward the land
Illahe . . . . .Land
Toto . . . . .Wind
Sick tum tum . . . . . .Sorrow, regret
An nah an nah . . . . .Surprise
Killipie . . . . .Capsize
Kockshet . . . . . .Fight, break, injure.
Sick . . . . .Sick
Elip . . . . .First
Alta . . . . .At present
Alkey . . . . .Afterwards
Hi you . . . . .Plenty
Konaway . . . . .All
Kar . . . . .Where
Till . . . . .Heavy
Delate . . . . .Straight
Seepy . . . . .Crooked
Hyack . . . . .Quick
Klawa . . . . .Slow
Chee . . . . .New

Dly . . . . .Dry
Koory . . . . .Run
Chaco . . . . .Come
Clatawa . . . . .Go
Mamook . . . . .Work
Kloshe . . . . .Good
Masatchy . . . . .Bad
Le Job . . . . .Devil
La plate . . . . .Priest
Lo lo . . . . .Carry
Pooh . . . . .Shoot
Kow . . . . .Tie
Klack . . . . .Untie
Hee hee la ma . . . . . .Gamble
Kumtux . . . . .Understand
Wake Konsick . . . . . . .Never
Konsick . . . . .How much
Kultus . . . . .Nothing
Kopet . . . . .Stop
Kopet waw waw . . . . . . .Stop talking
Nanitch . . . . .Look, see
Halo . . . . .None
Potlatch . . . . .Give
Iscum . . . . .Take
Klapp . . . . .Find
Ipsoot . . . . . . .Conceal, hide
Yawa . . . . .There
Yakwa . . . . .Here
Tum tum . . . . .Heart
Marcie . . . . .Thanks

Hee hee . . . . .Laugh
Tance . . . . .Dance
Tin tin . . . . .Music
Quonisum . . . . .Always
Wah . . . . .Astonishment
Kaata . . . . .Why
Pe kata . . . . .Why
Abba . . . . .Well there

Moosum . . . . .Sleep
Chick chick . . . . . .A wagon
Oiho . . . . .Sandwich Islands
Oakoak . . . . .This or that
Ikta . . . . .What
Tikke . . . . .Want
Ikta mika tikke, ...What do you want
Dly top seu . . . . .Hay
Snass . . . . .Rain
Cold snass . . . . .Snow
Le hash . . . . .Axe
Opsu . . . . .Knife
La Queen . . . . .Saw
La peep . . . . .Pipe
Kianoose . . . . .Tobacco
La plash . . . . .A plank
Kull kull stick . . . . .Oak
La plash stick . . . . . . .Cedar
Le gum stick . . . . .Pine
Kokwa . . . . .The same
Ikt stick . . . . .A yard
Tenass musket . . . . . . .Pistol
Poleally . . . . .Powder
Kalidon . . . . .Shot or balls
Musket . . . . .Gun
Skullapeen . . . . .Rifle
Mimaloose . . . . .Kill
Pooh . . . . .Shoot
Kapswallah . . . . .Steal
La Selle . . . . .Saddle
La breed . . . . .Bridle
Sitlie . . . . .Stirrup
Lesibro . . . . .Spurs
La pushmo . . .Saddle blanket
Siskiyou . . . . .Bob-tail
Leky . . . . .Spotted or piebald
De creme . . . . .Cream colored
Klale . . . . .Black

Top seu . . . . .Grass
Halluck laporte . . . .Open the door
Iktpooy laporte . . . . .Shut the door.
Klakany . . . . . . .Out of doors
Ancutty . . . . .Long ago
Lay lay . . . . .A long time
Mokook . . . . . .Barter, buy or sell
Keek wully coat . . . .Petticoat
Keekwully sikolocks Drawers
Lemoro . . . . .Wild
Ae kik . . . . .Fish hook
Staetejay . . . . .Island
Kooy kooy . . . . .Rings
Pe chuck . . . . .Green
Pill . . . . .Red
Te kope . . . . .White
Hyas Sunday . . . . .Christmas and Fourth of July

Klonass . . . . .I don't know
Kumtux . . . . . . .Understand
Wake nika kumtux . . . . . .I do not understand.
Midlight . . . . .Sit down

Midwhit . . .Stand up, get up
Laporte . . . . .Door
Halluck . . . . .Open
La Woolitch . . . . .A bottle
Iktpooy . . . . .Shut
Pil pil . . . . .Blood
Pilton . . . . .Fool
Klamenewhit . . . . .False
Tamanass . . . . . .Witchcraft
Klemenwhit . . . . .False
Cold . . . . .A year
Moon . . . . .Moon
Klakcee . . . . .Stars
How . . . . .Listen
Leglow . . . . .Nail
La chaise . . . . .Chair
Oskan . . . . .Cup
Lapell . . . . .Spade
Closhe Illahe . . . . . . .Prairie
Cold sun . . . . .Winter
Warm sun . . . . .Summer
Six . . . . .Friend
Shetsham . . . . .Swim
Wicht . . . . .Also
Tickachey . . . . .Although
Teilacoom . . . . . . .A relative
Momok Chaco . . . . .Bring

Numerals

Ikt 1
Mox .2
Klone 3
Locket 4
Quinam 5
Tahum 6
Sinimox 7

Sootkin 8
Quies 9
Totilum 10
Totilum pe ikt 11
Totilum pe mox 12
Ikt Tokamonak 100
Ikhyass Tokamonak 1000

Points of Compass

Stowbelow . . . . .North
Stegwaak . . . . .South
Sun chako . . . . .East
Sun midlight . . . . .West

Tyee Jimmy

Chief Tyee Jimmy of the Lillooet tribe, who lived on the Lillooet Rancherie, insisted on a clean rancherie and encouraged his people to be clean and to take pride in their homes. He also made sure that there was no carousing. Each house was surrounded by a beautiful garden, and the owners put many of their white neighbours to shame. Chief Jimmy and his people were Christians and attended church every night. They were happy and industrious and proud of their homes and way of life.

But Chief Jimmy once lost face with his people through a misunderstanding of the white man's law. Two Indians, Moses Paul and Paul Spintlum, murdered a white man in Williams Lake. They escaped and travelled down to Clinton, where they set up camp outside of town. Indians of the district knew they were there, but when questioned denied knowledge of them. The escapees were excellent woodsmen and could travel leaving no more trail than a ghost.

A thousand men were involved in a costly manhunt which continued for weeks. The authorities then appealed to the Kamloops tribe of the Shuswap Indians to join the hunt. This request was most unusual, but the murder had been a brutal one and the whole countryside was upset. The white community considered the two Indians to be very dangerous, and the Indians felt that all of their people were being discriminated against because of Spintlum and Paul. The Shuswaps agreed to aid in the search, and sent twelve trackers. Guards were posted in strategic places, but although the two Indians were sighted from time to time, they always disappeared, leaving no trace.

On one occasion a white man who was hunting horses, stumbled upon their camp while they were hiding in the forest near Clinton. They fed and treated him well, but asked him not to reveal their camp. He agreed to keep their secret, but instead went straight to the Clinton police to report their whereabouts. A posse was formed and surrounded the Indians' camp. The site was empty, and as the men rifled through it, a shot from the bush, presumably from the gun of one of the hunted men, killed a policeman.

After three months of failure, the police asked Tyee Jimmy to help them. Jimmy, as chief of the Lillooets, was popular with the other tribes, and his agreeing to help would win the co-operation of most Indians. The authorities showed him an old legal paper stating that the Indians should turn over their own people if they disobeyed the law. Tyee Jimmy wanted his people to be law-abiding, so he agreed to help after being promised that the two Indians would get a fair trial. Using the moccasin telegraph (the Indian "grapevine") he sent out word to Moses Paul and Paul Spintlum. It was not long before they came in to Lillooet, and Chief Jimmy took them to the police. After a quick trial, they were both convicted, and one was hanged at once. The other was given a sentence of life imprisonment, and when sentence was pronounced he said, "You hanged the wrong man. I did it."

Tyee Jimmy had understood that a "fair trial" meant that the men would not be hanged, but would be punished if found guilty. He had trusted the white authorities, but they had misled him. He vowed that he would never bring in another of his own people.

Chief Jimmy's honesty and faith in his people and his desire to help them were acknowledged by the homage paid him at his death. He had one of the largest and most impressive funerals ever held at the Lillooet Rancherie. Indians came from all over, and many white people attended his funeral. It was full ceremonial, with the Indians wearing wreaths and ashes on their heads and chanting the death song.

CHAPTER
3

The Reason They Came: Gold

The Golden Cache face

It was gold that attracted men to the colony of New Caledonia from California, Hong Kong, eastern North America and the British Isles. Although the only means of communication were letters delivered by ship and stagecoach, word spread rapidly and shiploads of gold-seekers poured into Victoria. They rushed to the gravel bars at Yale and from there, found their way to the interior by any means possible. The lure of instant wealth—a rich find, or even just a few nuggets in a goldpan—created such excitement that men could not get north fast enough.

The water wheel of the Arrastra equipment used to crush ore at the Lorne Gold mine

The Lorne Mine: John R. Williams

In 1862, John R. Williams, forebear of the present Russel family, came to B.C. from California. He walked from Yale to Quesnelmouth and continued to Pete Toy's Bar on the Finlay River in the Peace River country, prospecting there for some time. In 1870 he returned to Lillooet, where he prospected in summer and worked as a building contractor in winter.

Williams formerly had been a builder and operator of flour mills in Ontario. After he settled in British Columbia, he was contracted by the Hudson's Bay Company to build flour mills in areas where the population had concentrated and the need for flour was great. Flour was scarce and hundred pound sacks from Oregon cost $100. Williams built the mills at Dog Creek, the Cummings mill at Pavilion, and the Lillooet mill, later known as Marshall mill, at Cayoosh Creek.

About 1880 he married Mathilda Miller, whose family had come from Ontario to settle in Lillooet. Mathilda and John Williams never left Lillooet and here their six children, three boys and three girls, were born.

To the end of his days John Williams was a miner who loved prospecting for gold, and he made many "finds." In 1896, with friends Nat Coghland and William Young, he made his most important discovery—the Lorne Mine at Bridge River. The men operated this mine by the Arrastra method—using a water-wheel-driven ore-crusher—which technique Williams had learned in California. With his knowledge of water-wheel-driven flour mills, he was able to build an Arrastra at the Lorne Mine.

The Williamses' daughter Rachel married Joseph Russel in Lillooet around 1901. This union produced four girls and one boy, Len, who still lives in Lillooet. Before his marriage, Joseph Russel had been a prospector and miner. Together with William Allen he discovered the Pioneer Mine. In 1902 he sold the prospect for $250 and a grey horse, after being told by a mining engineer that it was no good. This mine, just one mile from the Lorne, became highly successful.

The Golden Cache: Arthur Noel

Names mysterious, facetious, hopeful or nostalgic were given to mines and claims by their owners. Some mines became world-famous and attracted money from far and near as their stocks were sold.

One version of the discovery of the Golden Cache is that a hunting party was climbing the mountain and one man had with him his Indian wife. During the climb she picked up an interesting piece of rock and showed it to him later. He was greatly impressed and staked the claim secretly and in the dark. Then he and his wife took off in haste during the night to record the claim as soon as the office opened.

A report in the *Province*, 27 January 1934, tells a different story after an interview with Arthur Noel, who was a respected prospector and miner in the district:

One Sunday morning back in 1895 when Noel was employed at the Bonanza Mine, the blacksmith on the property, Joe Copeland, showed Noel some quartz specimens of extraordinary richness. Gold was sticking out. The thought occurred to Noel that there perhaps might be placer gold in Cayoosh Creek. For days Noel and Copeland discussed the subject. They said nothing to the others.

One Sunday they started to prospect in Cayoosh Creek which had for years been placer mind for gold. The Chinese first mined the banks of the creek after the white miners had passed it up for richer bars on the Fraser. Hundreds of thousands of dollars worth of gold were taken from this creek. There was never an exact accounting, as the miners did not turn over all their gold to the Commissioner as is evident in Gold Commissioner F. Soues' Report of November 77/83.

Copeland knew little about prospecting, but Noel, using the knowledge gained in other districts, combed Cayoosh Creek, hoping to find the source of the rich "float." They continued all Sunday up the creek and were finally rewarded with the discovery of the quartz vein in a perpendicular ledge almost opposite the Bonanza Mine. As it was getting dark they returned to camp, but were back at "their find" early in the morning. It took nearly all day to "stake" their location in this rugged terrain. They called it "The Golden Cache," and when Mrs. Robert Carson of Pavilion sent her brother, George Magee, in Vancouver, a sample of the rich ore, he contacted J.M. McKinnon. In great haste they went to Lillooet to view "the find," were more than satisfied with its potential, and at once paid Noel and Copeland $25,000.00 cash. They formed "Golden Cache Mines Ltd."

Arthur Noel was in charge of the operations at the Golden Cache. Many engineers praised the property but when it was decided to put in a treatment plant early in the development, Noel objected, stating "it was not developed sufficiently to justify a milling plant." Contrary to his advice the plant was installed, and he quit his job.

Several managers and directors took over the development of this valuable property. The publicity boosted the stock prices on the Vancouver market, but it was successful for only a short time. Arthur Noel blamed "poor judgement and incompetence of management" for the failure of the Golden Cache. Following a spectacular robbery at The Cache, the public lost faith in the management. Stock prices, which had started at five cents and rocketed to two dollars, plummeted, and the mine closed. In 1897 it was re-opened by a Toronto company, but closed again in 1901. It was again opened in 1904 and "abandoned finally in 1910." In 1928 Arthur Noel and W.C. Savage bought the property at a tax sale. Noel never lost faith in the Golden Cache and Bonanza properties, and he continued to study the geology of the district. He always felt that there wre still rich veins—rather continuations of the old veins—available for profitable development in the old Golden Cache and its neighbour, the Bonanza.

The Golden Cache mine and mill on Cayoosh Creek

The "Bonanza Ledge" is best described in the Annual Mining Report of 1889:

The Bonanza Ledge is about 8 miles from Lillooet and is reached by a trail along Cayoosh Creek through a wild, picturesque country—the rugged mountains standing out in bold relief. In contradiction to the appearance of the Nicola Valley, it did not look "too nice" for a mineral region. That noble bachelor element, Gold, has the characteristic of wandering off by himself to some lonely, almost inaccessible locality. The ledge lies on the edge of a horseback or ridge, rising up from the creek on an incline of about 50 deg.—the opposite bank being a precipitous bluff fully 2,000 ft. high.

Outcroppings of the ledge are to be seen along the ridge in many places, and the vein can thus be traced for a long distance up the mountain, running about northwest by southwest.

Although the life of these two mines was short, news of the rich quality of the Bonanza and Golden Cache attracted prospectors and miners who looked farther afield and made other discoveries in the Bridge River area.

Bralorne: Delina C. Noel

On 29 July 1900, Mrs. Delina Noel arrived at Bridge River after a packtrain journey (with twenty-eight pack horses) by way of Seton and Anderson lakes and through McGillivray Pass. It was the beginning of a rich and colourful life, and she was to become as well known as her husband Arthur.

Delina Noel, the daughter of Overlander Joseph L'Itallienne, was born in Lillooet. She and her sister were educated in Quebec, but returned with their mother to Lillooet in 1896. On 14 December 1899 Delina married Arthur Noel, and they were to spend the greater part of their lives in the Bridge River District.

When Delina Noel arrived, she wanted to learn all about mining, so she visited the diggings. Her husband's crew of miners threatened to quit, as it was considered bad luck to have women at the mines. Arthur declared that every last one of them could quit if he liked, but Mrs. Noel was authorized by him to inspect the working face. The threatened exodus failed to materialize and in a short time Delina became a most welcome visitor, the men delighting to help her.

In 1902 she became mill superintendent of her husband's Bend'Or ten-stamp mill. Although never actually an underground miner, she acted as "top man" in one shaft-sinking project. In 1909 she carried her own gold brick to the old assay office on Hastings Street in Vancouver, travelling to the coast by horse-drawn BX stage. She also carried the mail and transported men and supplies by buckboard from Gun Creek to Pioneer.

During World War I she operated the five-stamp mill on the Lorne property. Miners were hard to find this time, and Delina went to Vancouver to seek men who would work the mine. Her judgement was shrewd. Of the five men she selected from the large number of unemployed men available, her choices proved to be expert miners; even more notable, none left his job in the following two years.

Another time she had to go to Vancouver to obtain blasting powder. She wanted to have the cargo barged to Britannia, but when the PGE railroad found out the nature of the shipment they refused to carry it on the passenger train. Delina Noel was not one to be easily put off. She persuaded the conductor to communicate with the railroad headquarters, and after the train had been held up for several hours, permission was given.

Delina was a lady of means; she and her husband Arthur purchased the Pioneer Mine and later sold it for $25,000 plus a one-quarter interest to Judge Williams and the Ferguson Brothers of Victoria. In 1910 they sold the Bend'Or to the Hon. James Dunsmuir (former premier and later Lieutenant Governor of B.C.) and his partner for $100,000 and stock—"without even a request for examination of the ground." These were very large amounts of money then.

An astute business person, Delina Noel never overlooked small details. Once, after she and a partner had explored a shaft, they sealed it and secured it with a fifteen-cent padlock. Claim jumpers restaked her claim, and in opening the eighteen-foot sealed shaft broke the lock. When the litigation was settled, included in the amount of $5,000 was the "cost" of the broken padlock.

The Arthur Noel home

Besides being an expert in the mining field, she was an excellent marksman who competed with the men in a favourite camp sport, target shooting. On a hunting trip, her husband once suggested she try a shot at a goat and on her first try she shot the goat through the heart. She was to become well known as a big-game hunter, and was credited with shooting an 800-pound grizzly. Large bears were not uncommon but this one was huge. The animal measured nine feet from the tip of its nose to the tip of the tail; the front feet measured eight inches and the hind feet twelve inches. It was believed to have been the seventh largest recorded in the area.

Mrs. Noel not only hunted but also trapped and caught lynx, rabbit, mink, and coyote. She was particularly proud of a mink coat, every pelt of which was trapped by herself. A fox pelt was once bartered to a prospector in payment for an important mineral claim.

Delina Noel's keen interest in mining continued to the end of her days, and she lived at

The Pioneer Mine equipment on Cadwallader Creek, including Arrastra crusher

Bralorne for many, many years. She maintained one of Vancouver's higher-class apartments on a year-round basis but she spent at least half her time in the hills of her beloved Bridge River district. As long as Mrs. Noel came back to prospect in the area in the summer season, her house in Bralorne was a landmark. The log house, built in 1916 to her specifications, boasted a very unusual fireplace. She and "Big Bill" Davidson selected stones representative of the known rock formations in the area, such as granite, augite, diorite, quartz, serpentine and greenstone. These stones were obtained from the old Arrastras in the Cadwallader Valley. The gold and other precious metal in the rock was hacked out by curiosity seekers after Mrs. Noel vacated the cabin and moved to Vancouver.

To honour Delina and Arthur Noel, Dr. W.S. McCann of the Geographical Survey of Canada in 1919 named Noel Mountain and Noel Creek after them. In 1958, British Columbia's centennial year, Delina Noel was presented with the Governor General's Medal. She was seventy-eight years old, but was still so active that she was reluctant to spare the time from the development work on a copper-tungsten project eight miles beyond Pioneer Mines in McGillivray Pass to journey to Lillooet for the presentation of the medal.

In front of Haylmore cabin: Will Haylmore, second from right

Will Haylmore:

The Bridge River attracted characters, and one was Will Haylmore. He was there in the days when the Bralorne area was known as Southfork-Goldbridge, and before the days of the Mission Mountain road. The placer miners brought their gold to Lillooet via the Bridge River Canyon Trail; it was a long walk and Will Haylmore claimed to have done all ninety miles of it in twelve hours. He walked with an easy gait in long strides and few people could keep up with him.

He was a tall, dignified Englishman, always immaculate in dress, with white shoulder-length hair combed back from his forehead. His friend Bob Bohemier thought that Haylmore looked like the handsome Wild Bill Cody (Buffalo Bill) and often tried to photograph him in a pose similar to Cody's, but Haylmore always declined.

Will Haylmore lived in the Bridge River area for fifty-four years and although he came to love it as his native country, a Union Jack always flew from the flagpole on his property. In his latter days he designated the signpost at Goldbridge which pointed to his home "Hyde Park Corner" to honour his birthplace in London.

He came to Canada when he was seventeen years old, and started with the CPR. He worked his way across the continent and down to California, where he heard of the gold rush at Barkerville in British Columbia. He came north and enroute stopped at the Martley ranch, "The Grange." Here he met a pretty girl who was so shy she only peeked around door corners when strangers stopped by. Maude Manson, daughter of Alice Maude (Martley) and W.G.C. "Billy" Manson, was later to become his wife.

Haylmore returned little wealthier from the goldfields and in Lillooet built the first brickyard on the Santini property, now Pritchard Flats. He manufactured bricks (not the adobe bricks made earlier by a Mexican) and sold them locally. He also built a house, which is part of the present Legion building. While living in Lillooet during the mining season Haylmore spent many winters in California. In fact, he walked the entire distance to California and back a number of times.

After the Manson family moved to the Riverview ranch in Lillooet, Will and the shy Maude were married on 13 December 1910, in St. Mary's Anglican Church. During their first years together they prospected Anderson and Seton Lakes, camping, as Mrs. Haylmore said, "on practically every available level piece of shore-line." They were not successful as prospectors, although they did have one promising claim above Shalalth.

Prospecting intrigued the Englishman, and he loved the mountains and wild country. On the job he wore heavy boots and socks which he pulled up over his pants; his undershirt sleeves showed below his shirt cuffs. But ever dapper, he always wore a white silk neckerchief.

A rocker at work, sifting tailings

Detail of a rocker

Haylmore continued to prospect in the Bridge River area, and owned the "Ida May," on Cadwallader Creek, until 1923. Later it became part of the Bralorne holdings. He became sub-mining recorder in the Bridge River District at a place adjacent to Goldbridge known to the natives as Southfork, and ran the government post office there. The site became known as Haylmore and was so designated on the map of British Columbia.

Will Haylmore was an avid gardener, and his house and office were surrounded with flower beds. He used rock to build walls around the perimeter, thus clearing the land and also giving a more formal appearance to the garden. In summer, the garden was a profusion of colour, and he even built a greenhouse to propagate plants alien to the region.

Inside the house was a white post on which he recorded the weather for many years. This record settled many an argument as to when the snow flew, when the freeze-up came, and when the swallows arrived and departed. Swallows were very special to him and he seemed to know just when to expect them.

He never stopped prospecting, and on one of his trips he discovered the Jewel Mine, which he was sure was a rich strike. The mineral was uranium. The first time he carried a sample out in his pocket, it actually burnt him, leaving a scar. The mine never amounted to much and he abandoned it. One time his friend Bob Bohemier visited him in his office and Will suddenly felt ill and asked, "Have you got any uranium on you?" Strangely, Bohemier had a sample in his pocket. Haylmore then explained that he had felt the powers of this element before, "But it took me some time to recognize the symptoms."

News of rich ore finds during the depression years brought many prospectors to the Bridge River area, and kept Will Haylmore very busy in the recording office. There were times a prospector would come in to file a claim but would not have the recording fee. Haylmore never turned him away but would pay the amount and tell the prospector, "You can work on my rock wall and work out the fee." He grubstaked many miners, but never became rich from their findings. Once, a claim was running out and the owner wanted it renewed, but had left it until the renewal deadline was almost up. Will Haylmore, as sub-mining recorder, had to get all recordings to the Lillooet office on time or the leases would expire. So he walked overnight along the road

42

The Haylmore greenhouse, unique in Lillooet

from Bridge River and Mission Mountain to Shalalth and in to Lillooet, arriving there in time to file at 9 a.m.

Haylmore enjoyed the solitude of mountain climbing, and was likely one of the first to conquer Mount Sloan. Although not a social man, he welcomed those who came to his door, and many citizens enjoyed his hospitality. Prominent mining men such as Dave Sloan, Austin Taylor, Victor Spencer, and Pat Mulcahyl, Deputy Minister of Mines, counted him as a friend.

his daughter Hilda remembers how in the early thirties her father was swamped with work. "Prospectors were lined up outside the door before we could open in the morning," she said, "and we had difficulty finding time to eat and no time for cooking. We took turns going out for meals to Goldbridge, the nearest restaurant, so the office could remain open to accommodate the prospectors." All this recording was done by hand because Will Haylmore would not use carbon paper and would not have a typewriter on the place.

During the Depression, he got money for work crews at Haylmore. Forestry crews worked under

Young Hilda Haylmore in her father's garden

Will Haylmore, foreground, at opening of South Fork Bridge

Will Haylmore

his direction until the allotment was used up and no more was forthcoming from the government. Sometimes the men continued to work and Haylmore paid them from his own pocket just to keep them employed.

Haylmore also had the men cut wood for him. Once John Holgerson was sawing with an old, dull crosscut saw, and the work progressed slowly. Holgerson found a file and sharpened the tool, sawing the log in jig time and piling up a stack of wood. When Will saw the great amount of wood he asked what had happened and John told him that he had filed the saw and improved it. Said the Englishman, "I'm very put out with you for filing the saw. With a dull saw I got more work and less wood."

during his fifty-four years in the Bridge district he watched countless mines open and close, including Forty Thieves, Why Not, Black Jack, Winnipeg, Brandon, Waterloo, Silver Plate, Casino, Cosmopolitan, Wood Chuck Group, Alhambra, Night Hawk, Blackbird, Whale, Ample, Monarch and Countless.

While Will Haylmore worked hard and lived at Haylmore, his wife spent her winters in their home in Lillooet so that their daughter could go to school. They moved to Haylmore for the summers, helping out by cooking for the forestry crews and doing work around the office. Maude Haylmore was long one of Lillooet's most respected citizens, connected as she was with the Martleys of Pavilion on her mother's side and the Mansons of Lillooet on her father's. She was a quiet lady, always interested in her friends and her surroundings, and was a treasure trove of information on the history of Lillooet. Without her help, much of this book would not have been written. She died at the age of eighty-seven and is buried in the Lillooet cemetery.

Will lived his life at Haylmore until he became too ill to stay alone and his family brought him back to Lillooet. They looked after him until it was necessary for him to go to a nursing home in Kamloops, where he died on 21 January 1964. He was buried at Haylmore at his own request, on the land which had been such a great part of his life.

CHAPTER
4

Those Who Stayed: Farmers, Ranchers and Horsemen

W.G.C. (Billy) Manson at Little Gun Lake

The Manson Family

William George Cox (Billy) Manson was born at Alexandria in 1864. His father, William, was a trader with the HBC, and his grandfather was assistant to HBC Chief Factor Peter Skeen Ogden of Fort Astoria, having joined the company from Scotland when he was nineteen. Billy's mother was Adelaide Victoria Ogden, granddaughter of the renowned factor.

When old enough to strike out on his own, Billy worked around the Interior, eventually coming to Pavilion with his brother, Peter, to work for Robert Carson of Pavilion Mountain. There he met Alice Maude Martley, and both being excellent riders they rode together frequently. A romance soon blossomed, to the Martleys' consternation, for they still held to the old country belief that landed gentry married landed gentry and a young cowboy was not their idea of a son-in-law. The two young people were much in love, however, and one moonlit night they rode horseback into Clinton and were married. The family accepted the young couple. Billy continued to work on the Grange, where they lived for fourteen years until they had saved enough money to buy Riversdale Ranch in Lillooet at the confluence of Cayoosh Creek and Fraser's River.

Alice Maude Martley was a slim, pretty young girl, only five feet tall, with blue eyes and very blonde hair. She had learned to ride on the Grange and often rode to hounds at Ashcroft, where her half-sister (the daughter of Mrs. Martley by a former marriage) had married a Cornwall of Ashcroft Manor. These hunts were the highlight of Alice's life when she was young. She was fearless, and once rode a bucking horse side-saddle, earning the respect of the cowboys.

When the family moved to Riversdale, she took over the management of the ranch while

About 1900: Donald Manson and brother Tom, to his right

each day after lunch, undoubtedly a carryover from her landed gentry background. She enjoyed walking from the homestead to Lillooet to visit with her daughters, all of whom married and lived there. And she was adored by her sons-in-law, who admired her dignity and enjoyed her quick sense of humour.

Billy and Alice Maude's children, all born at the Grange, were Maude (Mrs. Will Haylmore); William Martley (Tom), who did not marry; and Donald Arthur, also a bachelor, who died overseas during World War I; Florence Marie, known as Floss (Mrs. Howard Dolph Reed, whose husband came to Lillooet from Ohio, and was one of the top three bridgemen in British Columbia); and Dora Virginia (Mrs. George Prosser, whose husband was a Lillooet businessman).

Billy Manson became known throughout the North American continent and Europe as an excellent shot and hunting guide who would guarantee game for his clients. Since hunting went on practically year round in those days, Billy soon devoted his full time to being a guide. His list of clients includes European aristocracy, the military, and big businessmen.

William Manson, Billy's father, had been educated in Scotland, graduating from Edinburgh University, and during his years with the HBC he taught school at various places in British Columbia. Billy was educated for the most part at home. Living at HBC posts as a child introduced him to many different types of people, and this was an asset to him in the guide business.

Billy Manson told many amusing tales of the

husband Billy was guiding hunters. She grew a beautiful flower garden around her elegant old log house, and her kitchen garden supplied the family with the year's supply of vegetables. With the help of her daughters Maude, Floss, and Dora, she cooked for the farm crews, and with her sons Tom (William Martley Manson) and Donald, she operated an orchard from 1921 to 1945. The main market for the several varieties of apples and pears was Vancouver, but each season she also shipped three carloads of 900 boxes each north to Quesnel and Williams Lake. She had a packing house on the property and a separate root cellar where she could store 200 to 300 boxes of apples. In 1945 she finally gave up the orchard, having been priced out of business.

alice Maude Manson was a woman of quiet dignity and although she wore work clothes while doing her chores, she always changed into a dress

Tom Manson, centre, with hunting party at Hawthorne Creek

European aristocracy who came to Lillooet to hunt for big game trophies. Many of his favourite stories centred around Baron Von Plessen, a German from Alsace Lorraine. The baron enjoyed hunting and was a good sport. His irritation was reserved for his manservant, Simmons, whom he brought along with him. Poor Simmons was frequently shouted at, and often he and the baron were in loud disagreement. A source of amusement to the packers and guides was a rubber bathtub which the baron insisted on bringing along. Simmons, although he was not good at cooking the baron's meals, cooked outdoors and the baron's reactions to some of his offerings were another source of amusement. Manson's men were very fond of the baron, and would pick pails full of huckleberries for him, a treat he appreciated.

In those days there were not regulated areas for guides; each hunted wherever he chose. So keen was Billy to satisfy his clients that when one group wanted the largest possible mountain sheep trophies, he arranged to take them to Jasper, Alberta, where the mountain sheep are bigger than the Lillooet species. His usual areas were the Hurley River, North Fork, and South Fork of the Bridge River to Churn Creek (the boundary of the Bridge and Chilcotin countries), the Shulap Range, and occasionally the Fountain and Big Bar country. The game was mainly mountain sheep, mule deer, goats, grizzlies and black bears.

It was a sight to see the Manson outfit starting out on a hunt from Lillooet. The many pack horses, help, and the clients on their fine saddle ponies were led by sons Tom and Donald, with Billy riding along with the guests. Clients were allowed to shoot only two of any species; the Mansons were well known as conservationists and refused to take out those who were not, no matter how influential they were.

So famous was the shooting prowess of Billy Manson that the Savage Gun Company used his picture in an advertisement for their .303 rifle. He posed in his hunting outfit—a handsome fringed buckskin jacket decorated with grizzly bear claws down the sides of the neck opening, fringed buckskin pants, moccasins, and a cartwheel hat—standing with his gun. The caption read, "The Man Behind the Savage." In the late 1890s, in the hills above Little Gun Lake and using a 45.70 repeater rifle, he shot the largest grizzly bear

From left to right: "Billy" Manson, Tom Manson, Donald Manson, Indian packer.

THE MAN BEHIND THE SAVAGE

ever killed in the territory up to that time. It measured ten feet, six inches.

Tom Manson remembers his father, Billy, as a stern disciplinarian who saw to it that his boys learned to work very early in life. Although he gave his sons horses, it was with the understanding that as they earned money, they would pay him for them. Tom started going out with the hunting parties when he was thirteen years old and became a well-known guide in his own right.

tom is a tall, handsome man at age ninety. He continued to live on the home place, Riversdale, until 1973 when he moved uptown to live with his niece Hilda Haylmore. Except for service overseas during World War I, he lived all of his life around Lillooet. Born on the Grange on 13 May 1885, he remembers at age nine seeing the last of the ox-teams come into Ashcroft. There were two wagons, each pulled by a twelve-ox team. The beasts were hitched together with a heavy timber yoke, and the driver walked beside the team with a long whip.

Tom was an excellent horseman and as a boy he drove his father's horses over the mountains on the west side of the Fraser to the McDonald Ranch on Watson Bar, which was below Big Bar on "Fraser's River." When he was a young man he drove horses into the Bridge River at a time when all the traffic went out Cayoosh Creek and down to

Shalalth on Seton Lake, then over Mission Mountain into the Bridge River country. The long, tough trip was made for seventy-five cents per head.

He was also an excellent tracker and he could read trail better than some of the natives. He was hired as a guard during the manhunt for the Indian murderers Moses Paul and Paul Spintlum.

Tom Manson guided until the 1950s. He is the last of Billy Manson's family since the death in 1971 of his sister, Mrs. Maude Haylmore.

Manson Mountain, Manson Creek and Manson Harbour are named after this distinguished pioneering family.

The Martleys of "The Grange"

One of the earliest ranchers on Pavilion Mountain was Captain John Martley, a well-educated man whose father had been a judge of the Landed Estates Court of Dublin. For many years Martley served his country as a professional soldier, fighting with one of the Irish regiments throughout the Crimean War.

Maria, Mrs. John Martley, with her son Arthur H. J. Martley

Haylmore family collection

He emigrated to British Columbia with his English wife and their two children, Arthur and Isabelle, arriving in New Westminster on 15 May 1861. Unfortunately the family's belongings were all lost when the ship on which they were being transported foundered on Race Rocks in the Strait of Juan de Fuca.

Although Captain Martley was one of three Imperial Army officers permitted by military grant to acquire land in the interior of the province, he turned down the grant after learning of the distance and difficulties of getting his family into the Okanagan Valley where the land was situated. Instead, he chose to go to Lillooet.

The route that the Martley family travelled to reach Lillooet was the same one the miners were taking to the goldfields. Starting from New Westminster, they went by steamer to Harrison Lake, up the lake to Port Douglas, then over the Royal Engineers' road and portages (where the children were carried in panniers on the backs of horses), across Anderson and Seton lakes on steamers, and on to Lillooet over the Cayoosh trail.

In Lillooet, they were invited to stay at the home of A.C. Elliott, Lillooet's second magistrate and later B.C.'s fourth premier. Mrs. Elliott was delighted to have visitors, as there were few white women neighbours to visit.

Captain Martley left his wife and children with the Elliotts while he looked for land. On Pavilion Plateau he found what he was looking for, a large piece of land partly on Pavilion Creek near Pavilion Lake, which was being farmed by David Reynolds, an American. Reynolds had been a squatter on the land for two years and had successfully grown vegetables there. When Lieutenant Mayne passed through Pavilion in 1858 he wrote: "I saw the American Reynolds using a plow, the first I had seen in B.C." He must have been a good farmer, for he grew oats, barley, turnips, garden vegetables, and potatoes, which he sold to the miners. Some of his turnips weighed over fifteen pounds and he produced 375 bushels of oats to the acre.

Martley pre-empted 460 acres of this land for himself, his wife, son, and daughter and was Crown granted the Reynolds property after Reynolds left. The combined properties formed a fine ranch.

The captain built a home for his family and named it "The Grange," after a previous home in the old country. As there was not yet a road into the area, he brought his wife and children from Lillooet on horseback. Mrs. Martley was surprised to find ranchers on the route up the mountain. It seemed to her that every flat of meadowland already had a house and some cattle. At 12 Mile Barnard Sallus, for whom Sallus Creek at 14 Mile was named, and Joseph L'Itallienne were ranching. At 15 Mile were William Brown, George

Bailey, and George Tinker. At 17 Mile William H. Clarke and John Currie held a pre-emption. Joseph Watkinson was at 18 Mile. Thomas Cole was at 18 Mile and John A. Cameron at 20 Mile. Later Robert Carson, Michael Gillen, Phillip Cullen, Freeman Clarke, and Louis Eholt ranched on Pavilion Mountain, and John L. Hughes and William Lee settled on Pavilion Creek.

His military bearing, direct, piercing eyes, curly hair, mutton-chop sideburns and goatee all gave him a commanding appearance.

Mrs. Martley was impressed with the beauty of her surroundings—the big open meadow where the house stood near the road, guarded by Pavilion and Tom Cole mountains, and the winding creek which supplied them with clean, clear water from beautiful Pavilion Lake. In summer the lake was surrounded by a band of green poplars which later turned golden.

Not only had Mrs. Martley never pioneered before, she had never done her own cooking. This might have been a calamity, but she was rescued by a Mrs. Mallon, who, en route to Barkerville, stayed at the Grange long enough to teach Mrs. Martley to cook over an open fireplace. For several years, this was how Mrs. Martley did her cooking.

As Lieutenant Mayne had observed, Indians were impressed with any touch of the military, and the Indians of Pavilion were no exception. Captain Martley gained their respect at once. His military bearing, direct, piercing eyes, curly hair, muttonchop sideburns and goatee all gave him a commanding appearance. The Indians wanted to emulate him, and as his name was John, they wanted to be called John too. To please them, Mrs. Martley called each one Johnny. As she came to know them she gave special names to each. She called the old chief "William the Conqueror" and he became known as "Old Bill." An old Indian living in Marble Canyon was "Charles the Bold," and later became known as "Canyon Charlie."

One time when her husband was away, a group of Indians with their chief, Teemkin, stopped at the Grange and came inside to warm themselves by the fireplace. Indians were always welcome at the Grange, and Mrs. Martley was not alarmed by their arrival. One, however, became too friendly and put his hand on her shoulder. This gesture was unusual, as the local Indians had always showed Mrs. Martley great respect. Incensed by this familiarity, she took up a broom and chased them all out the door.

Because it was on the stage route, freighters and stages used to stop there, providing Mrs. Martley and the family with work as well as visitors.

The Grange was always a busy place. It covered nearly 1,000 acres, and the activities which took place there included land clearing, haymaking and tending 800 sheep and some cattle. The sheep and cattle were slaughtered at the ranch and taken to Lillooet by wagon and packhorse, or sent directly to the mines over the road built by the Royal Engineers. The miners at Barkerville were always glad to get fresh meat and were willing to pay well for it. The Grange also sent butter, chickens, potatoes, turnips and carrots to Barkerville.

Mrs. Martley contributed to the family coffers by raising turkeys, which also went to the mines. They were a welcome change from beef, lamb and wild game, and commanded a good price.

Mrs. Martley dressed, plucked, cleaned and wrapped the birds in clean cloth before shipping. One fall she had forty large turkeys dressed and ready to be shipped when word came from the mines that they had closed for the winter. She wrapped the turkeys well and put them in a snowbank to preserve them; this could have been the first deepfreeze in B.C. The family had their fill of turkey that winter, and Maude Haylmore could never remember her mother, Alice Maude (Martley) Manson, later having turkey for the traditional Christmas dinner.

Captain John Martley was also in the freighting business; he owned two or three freight wagons, each pulled by a six-horse team. His son Arthur freighted from Ashcroft to Lillooet in the very good time of two days, from Ashcroft to the Grange through Marble Canyon in one day, and then from the Grange to Lillooet in another. An Indian named Johnny Edwards (brother of Chief Edwards of Pavilion's 22 Mile Reserve) drove one of the Martley teams.

Mrs. Martley's first child in British Columbia was born in quite a different fashion from her confinements in Ireland. She rode horseback down the steep mountain trail, intending to stay with her friend, Mrs. Elliott. However, when it was discovered that the Elliott's daughter Mary had scarlet fever, she went to the only other available place, the doctor's own house. Dr. Featherstone, Lillooet's first doctor, had a cabin above the present post office location, and here, with an Indian woman to keep house, he looked after his patients. While Mrs. Martley was in labour it rained, and the roof above the bed leaked. Being a man used to emergencies, Dr. Featherstone brought Mrs. Martley an umbrella to hold. Thus Alice Maude Martley was born on 5 October 1862, under an umbrella, in Dr. Featherstone's cabin in Lillooet.

Alice Maude married Billy Manson, a member of another Lillooet pioneer family. Arthur Martley, the family's only son, was well known throughout the Cariboo as a freighter, rancher, and poet. Two daughters of Mrs. Martley by a former marriage came from England to the Grange and married into families in the area: Cerise Ayr married Caspar Phair and her sister married Henry Cornwall of Ashcroft.

The Grange was the Martley family's only home, and Captain John Martley was buried there. Mrs. Martley lived on at the ranch with Arthur until 1899, when it was sold to the Brysons. Then she moved to Lillooet, where she lived with her son until her death in 1910. She was buried beside her husband, and their graves are marked on the Grange land, which is now known as the Lower Ranch.

Arthur Hugh John Martley

The Carsons of Pavilion

in 1863 a young Scotsman, Robert Carson, fell in love with a stretch of grassland on Pavilion Mountain and carved there a homestead which was to become one of the best known ranches in the Cariboo. It was a stopping place for stages and travellers going north and for those coming from the east via the Marble Canyon.

Carson was born in Edinburgh in 1841. An orphan, he came to the United States at the age of nineteen, and joined a wagon train crossing the United States. In Colorado, the train was attacked by Indians, and although the wagons in front of and behind Carson's were lost, his miraculously was left untouched. He continued to California, where he heard of the gold rush in British Columbia and headed north through Boise, Idaho, entering Canada in the Okanagan and travelling north through Kamloops to the mines at Quesnelmouth.

Once in the mining district, this astute young Scotsman saw the need for pack trains and set about acquiring animals. Except for a short sojourn in Washington, Carson continued to pack supplies to the goldmines for many years, eventually packing out of Lillooet.

During the time that his base was in Lillooet, Carson travelled over the Pavilion Mountain road looking for feed for his animals, and found the flats where he was to settle. In 1867 he bought land and built his first log house. This ranch, known as the 26 Mile, commanded a magnificent view of mountain ranges. In summer the vista was of granite bluffs and peaks and of heavily forested mountains. In winter the mountains glistened white and shining as far as the eye could see. Carson could look down on the Grange (the Martley ranch) and east towards Marble Canyon. To the southeast the ranges rimming Hat Creek stood majestic on the horizon. The immediate view was of acres of grazing land and meadows, reaching over the 6,000-foot tops of the Pavilion mountains. Carson used the plentiful wood from his land to make artistic and effective Russel fences.

The grade to the north side of the mountain was an easy one, but travellers heading north in Carson's day found a twisting, narrow bed cut into

Slaughterhouses of Foley, Welch & Stewart on Seton Lake

the side of the hill with a series of steep switchbacks snaking through a thick forest of jackpine, spruce, and juniper. Halfway down, though, through a break in the trees there was a fine view of the clearing on the flats, and below, the perfectly shaped Pear Lake, named by the Royal Engineers when they first saw it. At the foot of Pavilion Mountain, the road flattened out and continued eastward to Kelly Lake, a beautiful blue-green body of water rimmed with grass and nestled between steep hills at an elevation of 3,505 feet. The meadows at the east end of the lake were a welcome sight, as they provided food and rest for the weary pack animals and good camping for the travellers.

With this ranch site chosen, Carson's first requirement was a steady supply of water. A ditch had been built on the land by Chinese miners, and he decided that he could use it for irrigation. His application for water rights on the creek stirred up a veritable war, for a neighbouring rancher named Clark objected to water being cut off from his property. He brought the matter to court, where the suit went on for some time, being carried, it is said, to the Privy Council. While the legal battles were being fought in court, war on the mountaintop was waged as Clark would cut the ditch and divert the water and Carson's men would patch the ditch and re-direct it. One cowboy on the Carson ranch was an old Indian named Pecullah Kosta, a big quiet , man.

When Pecullah thought that the nonsense about the water had gone far enough, he decided to patrol the water ditch himself. One night, watching quietly as a shadow, he saw a figure cutting the ditch. Sneaking up, he roped the man, who turned out to be one of Clark's friends, tied him up and took him back to Carson's barn. Next morning the police came from Lillooet for the man, but this was the last attempt at ditch cutting. Robert Carson eventually won his case, but Clark never forgave him, steadfastly refusing to sell him any land in later years.

Robert Carson built up a good herd of cattle and expanded his acreage by buying out other ranchers and applying for land grants. The only outlets for beef were through Clinton and over Fountain Mountain to Lytton, or northward up the Cariboo trail. Robert Carson was a strong supporter of a direct road from Lillooet to the coast, and he took part in the only cattle drive to use the Lillooet Trail.

During the winter after this famous drive, he tended his cattle on land on the north arm of the Fraser River, adjoining the farm of a family named Magee. There he met Eliza Jane, daughter of the owner, Hugh Magee. Their friendship blossomed and when spring came, Carson proposed and was accepted. Promising to return the following spring

Eliza Jane Carson at the Carsons' log house door

for their wedding, he started off for his home at Pavilion. The road through the Fraser Valley was long, and by the time he reached Hope he was a very lovesick cowboy. He turned his horse around and spurred him over the 100 miles back to the Magee farm in record time and persuaded Eliza Jane to marry him at once and return with him to Pavilion. The Magee family rose to the occasion and the marriage was performed at their home on 3 April 1878, by Gastown's Methodist minister, Rev. Thomas Derrick, nicknamed "Old Hoisting Gear." The happy newlyweds' two-week honeymoon took them from New Westminster by boat to Yale, then by stagecoach to the ranch.

When the stage carrying Robert and his bride arrived home, the first priority was a meal for the stagecoach passengers. On the sideboard stood the usual bottles of liquor offered with meals. After the meal, when the passengers were ready to depart, Eliza Jane put on her hat and coat as if ready to go with them. The new bridegroom was taken by surprise and asked where she was going. Pointing to the bottles, she replied, "Either they go or I do." Robert Carson, to the dismay of cowboys and passengers, took all the bottles outside and carefully smashed each one on a rock. That was the last time that liquor was seen in the Carson household, except for brandy which was kept for medicinal purposes. After this incident, Robert Carson never took another drink. He conducted

business in many places and was often told, "If you don't drink with the boys you will not get their business." To this he would reply, "I don't need the business if a drink will buy it."

The Carsons had ten children, five boys and five girls: Minnie Isabel (Mrs. John Bryson); William George; Helen Mary, called Ella (Mrs. John David McGuire); Eliza Jane, known as Girlie (Mrs. Henry Avery); Robert Henry (who was Liberal MLA for Kamloops and Speaker of the B.C. Legislature); Edith Linda (Mrs. Charles Pollard, who married into one of Clinton's oldest pioneering families); Frederick John (who ran freight wagons for Carson's Freight Lines); Ernest Crawford (Conservative MLA for Lillooet and Provincial Minister of Public Works), and Edna Ruth (Mrs. Edward Morris).

There was no school on Pavilion Mountain, but Mrs. Carson was determined that the children would have an education. She found that the government would supply books and a teacher if there were ten children in attendance. Mrs. Carson often boarded other children to keep the number up to ten. A log schoolhouse was erected at the fork in the road one and a half miles from the Carson home. Young Robert was delegated to ride his horse to school during the fall and winter months an hour before the others to light the fires, often riding through deep snowdrifts.

This school provided elementary education only, and it was not until W.J. Semple, principal of Columbian College in New Westminster, rode through the territory looking for pupils for the college that Mrs. Carson decided to send their eldest daughter, Minnie, to school there. At this time the college in New Westminster was affiliated with McGill University and the only school in B.C. to offer university entrance examinations.

The Carsons in later years

Because her home-made butter was sought after by those who passed by the ranch as well as by a storekeeper in Williams Lake, she saw the way to put aside an "education fund." She told her children that if they were willing to do the milking, she would make butter and sell it for cash to go into the fund. Milking forty head a day and skimming the cream by hand for churning was quite a chore as eventually Mrs. Carson got a Laval Separator, then a new device which the children turned by hand. To solve the problem of keeping large amounts of butter sweet and fresh, Mrs. Carson designed a cooler. A large box, forty feet by eight feet, made of heavy planks was lined with a metal box six inches smaller. Ice was packed beneath and around this metal box, which was known as "the dairy box." The dairy itself was a log cabin. The ice came from Pavilion Lake; cut in winter, hauled up the mountain by a wagon on sleigh runners, packed in sawdust, and kept in an icehouse for summer use.

The storekeeper at Williams Lake, Mr. Kelly, offered to take all the butter Mrs. Carson could make. She would not drop her regular customers, but agreed to sell all she could ship at his expense by express from Clinton. Since butter was a scarce commodity, and he could charge what he pleased, Kelly agreed to her terms. Four of the Carson children went to Columbian College on the proceeds from these butter sales.

Robert Carson believed that a job well done begot more business, and he brought up his sons to give their best. His hay was always put up carefully and he sold only the top quality. If he saw second-grade hay being loaded for a buyer, he would say, "Take that off, we have plenty of our own cattle to eat it." His grain received the same careful treatment; he always put it through a fanning mill to make sure it was extra clean before selling. Carson rose at 4 a.m. made the rounds of the ranch, then came in to the kitchen to sit and read, often by candlelight, until breakfast. He was equally rigid in his bedtime habits, retiring at 9 p.m. regardless of who was there.

Winter on Pavilion Mountain was a beautiful time with everything covered in snow, but it made living and working difficult. The wind was strong and temperatures would often drop to thirty degrees F below zero. To protect his young cattle, Carson bought a piece of land at High Bar, twelve miles below Big Bar on the Fraser and well below Pavilion ranch. Here the winters were milder and the young cattle could rustle feed rather than having to be fed. Come spring, the grass on the bar was the earliest in the country, and the hay there was ready long before the hay at Pavilion. After the first crop on the mountain was cut, a second crop at High Bar was ready for harvesting.

The quality of the feed grown on the mountain meadows was excellent, and Carson supplied the BX freight hauling teams with grain and hay. Steve Tingley, owner of the BX, not only hauled Carson's hay for customers but also carried it for his own animals on the Cariboo road, knowing that even though the price might be higher, he would get more work from his teams on Carson's feed.

Carson's horses were particularly well fed and well trained. When the first Lillooet bridge was being built and several outfits had failed to haul the heavy timbers, Carson was given the task and his animals got the job done on time.

There was no road from High Bar to the mountain road when Carson bought the ranch there. He applied to the government for a road, and when they refused, he went ahead, hired Chinese help, and put the road through himself.

The Carson ranch was known far and wide and was visited by many B.C. officials. Methodist, Presbyterian and Anglican ministers held services in the Carson home.

Eventually, the Carson ranch was sold to the Bryson family, and later to Colonel Spencer; it is still one of the most active ranches in this territory.

The Kanes of the "Box K"

Captain James Kane was an Irishman who sailed around the Horn en route to the new Colony of British Columbia, landing in New Westminster in 1860. He arrived in a ship of which he was half owner, having heard about the rich goldfields in the Colony and the great need for shipping and transportation. Captain Kane's enquiries into the possibilities of freighting up the river resulted in his selling his share of the large vessel and buying a smaller one, the *Scuddy*. This he used to move freight upriver from New Westminster to Yale, which was then the end of water transportation. His business was brisk, as the miners upriver needed supplies and had gold to be transported back.

Yale was a district seat of government and a bustling town filled with miners, drifters, gamblers, and opportunists; it had twelve saloons and one magistrate. It was here that Captain Kane met Christine, a beautiful Indian girl, whose family lived near Yale, and they were married in 1861. On 19 September 1863, a son, Billy, was born.

James Kane could not long ignore the excitement of the gold rush, and when Billy was two years old, his father went north to make his fortune. He never returned, and word sifted through to Christine that he had made a rich strike and was murdered for his new-found wealth. This news was never substantiated, and his grieving wife waited three years for him to return. In 1868, when Billy was five years old, Christine met and married a freighter named Richley. Needing pasture for his mules, Richley bought 14 Mile ranch on the Lytton-Lillooet trail, and in 1877 the family moved from Yale and started to ranch. Billy was then fourteen and loved the life immediately as he was passionately fond of animals.

Billy grew into a strong young man, six feet tall, and moved with a slow, easy grace which stamped him as a natural horseman. When he was sixteen he built with his own hands a log barn that still stands on the homestead—now known as Pine Grove ranch. At eighteen, Billy wanted a place of his own and bought out George Baillie at

Young "Billy" Kane, 1891

A. Murchin photograph

20 Mile. He worked hard to make 20 Mile into a fine ranch suitable for the family he hoped to have with Susan Watkinson, daughter of neighbour Joseph Watkinson of Watkinson's Bar. A romantic young man, Billy expressed his feeligs for Susan in letters and poetry. In 1882 the two were married in the Watkinson home by Archdeacon Small, and returned to 20 Mile ranch with its vista of the Fraser river winding its way down the Lillooet-Lytton trench.

It was a happy marriage and produced eight children, seven sons (James, William Herbert, Ernest, Walter Cecil, Joseph, Albert, Stanley) and one daughter (Susan). To educate these children Billy Kane, Fred Watkinson (Susan's brother), and Charles McGillivray built a school at Watkinson's Bar and hired a teacher. Education in this remote area was not always a continuous process: the boys helped when needed on the farm and the girls helped in the home during the harvesting season when there were many more mouths to feed. Three or four years of steady schooling constituted a good education.

Billy Kane was a hard worker. He took employment with the CPR when the Cisco Bridge near Lytton was being built. This was a veritable fortress of a structure with pillars of granite. Billy saved a man's life while on this job, and the CPR presented him with a gold watch for his valour. The wages that he earned bought the first cattle for his ranch, and he gradually built up a fine herd from this stock. His brand was a capital K inside a square box, and the ranch became known as the "Box K."

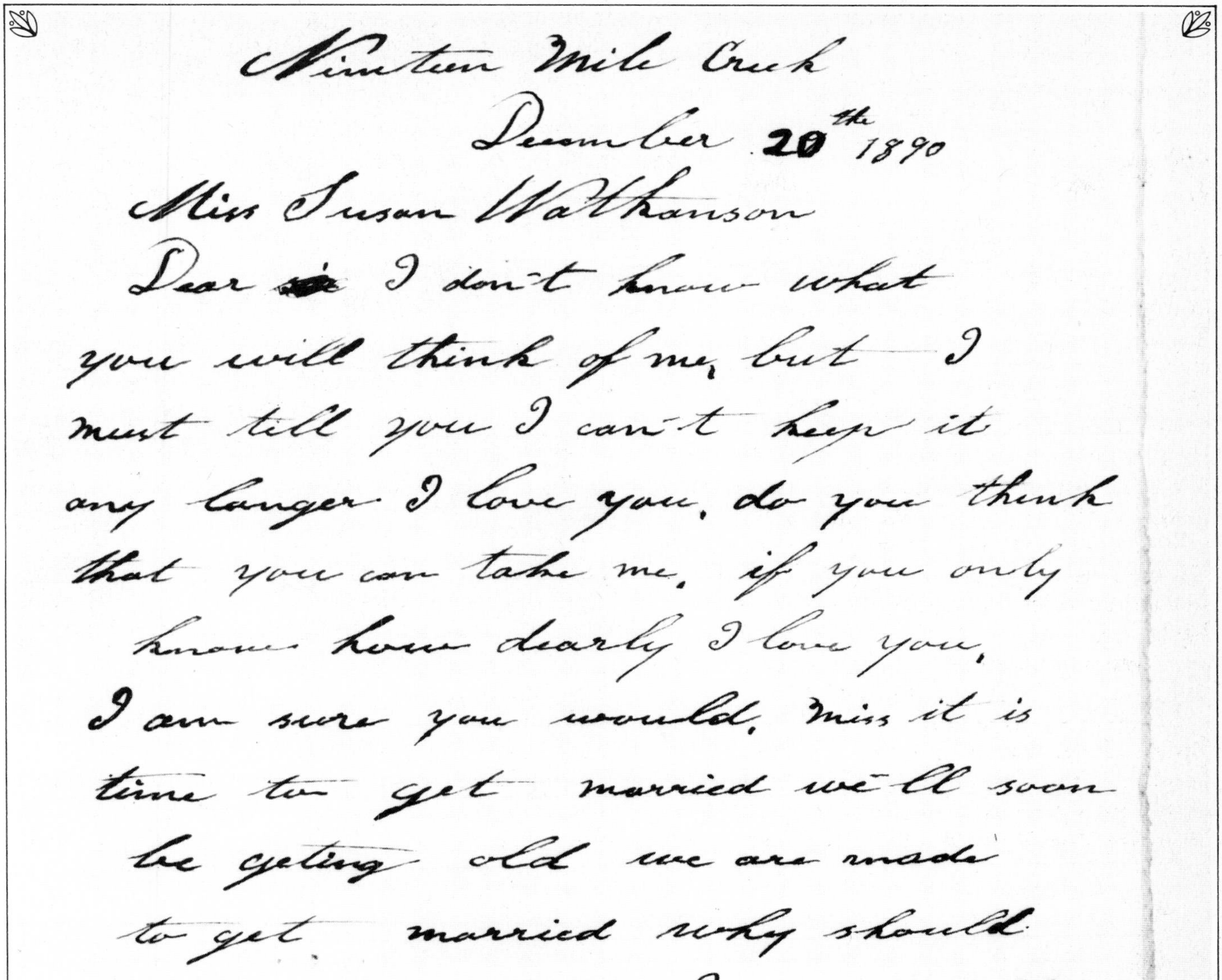

Nineteen Mile Creek

December 20th 1890

Miss Susan Wathanson

Dear sir I don't know what
you will think of me, but I
must tell you I can't keep it
any longer I love you. do you think
that you can take me. if you only
know how dearly I love you,
I am sure you would. miss it is
time to get married we'll soon
be geting old we are made
to get married why should
not get married, I never could
think of no one else but
you, and the only you are the first
one and the only one.

good-bye miss I will
see you some day
Yours respectfully,

Wm Kane

You will find
a silk handkerchief

Horseman Kane

In the 1890s he was raising, slaughtering and curing his own pork, and his bacon was much sought after. Local miners, including a group of Chinese miners who had a winter townsite on the river below the Box K, bought all of Kane's bacon, which sold at a dollar for six pounds. Each summer he raised fifty to sixty pigs, and sold them to the miners during the winter. He also butchered surplus cattle, which sold readily in Lillooet and Lytton. One fall, he drove his surplus of about fifty head over the mountains to Ashcroft, where he sold them to Pat Burns, well-known Lower Mainland butcher, at about forty dollars a head —a good price for that time.

Eventually Billy Kane owned and operated three farms—the 20 Mile, 18 Mile, and 14 Mile. By the 1930s, he and his son Bill, working together, shipped thirty tons of alfalfa seed to an Ontario buyer. This seed was known as Kane Alfalfa, and the cleaning mill used to clean the seed still stands on Kane's Acres. The Kanes owned the first haymower in the valley, brought from Lytton by boat up the Fraser before there was a road into the area.

Bill Kane tells a story about land values when land was there for the asking. His father, not having the time to work 18 Mile ranch, offered it to his brother-in-law, Fred Watkinson, for the taxes owing on it—which amounted to four

dollars. Fred's answer was: "I wouldn't give my hat for it!" Recently this farm was offered for sale at $200,000.

Billy's great love for horses kept him on the lookout for good stock. He ran a large and valuable string, and he was also expert at racing his horses. A special favourite was Platinum, a beautiful dark grey animal which held the half-mile record for Canada. Billy delighted in racing his horses across the country; no race was too small for him to enter. His horses ran in the competitions which were held on the main streets of Lillooet and Lytton, and he almost always came up with a winner.

One time Billy was riding on a mountain above his ranch when something startled his horse and he was thrown off. To his consternation he found that he had broken his leg. He realized that he would never get home unless he could get back on his horse. Pulling himself over to a tree with a low crotched branch, he situated himself so that he could get his heel well down into the crotch. Then, agonizing though it was, he pulled his leg straight, setting the break. He splinted it with branches and was finally able to pull himself up to a standing position. Although his horse was an extremely high-spirited animal which only Billy

Kane could ride, it sensed its master's predicament and stood close until Billy could mount. The trip home was excruciatingly painful, being entirely downhill through a rocky creekbed, but Billy gave the animal its head and it took him home.

Billy once had a worse ride than this one. He had shot a large buck and was about to "bleed" the animal. As he stepped astride the buck's neck, the deer suddenly jumped up and made three long leaps down the hill, the hunter's feet touching the ground each time. On the third leap the buck fell dead, and Kane fell off gladly.

Billy's excellent horsemanship was often put to the test. One time he was asked to saddle break a horse that had already killed a man because of its wild bucking. Billy took the animal home and turned it into a corral where he could observe it. When time came to saddle and ride the renegade, the horse did not buck at all—to everyone's amazement. Billy had observed the animal well, and had noted that a tight belly band drove this horse wild. His secret was a loose cinch.

He was an expert farrier and reset his horses' shoes every two weeks. Once when cattle broke through the garden fence, Billy ran out, shod one of his horses, chased the offending cattle back into the field, then removed the horse's shoes and turned him loose.

Another of his favourite stories told of prospecting in the Cascade mountains on the west side of the Fraser and hearing his horse scream. Gold pan in hand, he ran to see what was happening and found a grizzly bear about to attack his saddle mare. He grabbed a stick and began to beat the pan. Startled by the din, the bear took off. Billy remembers that he and his horse camped together near the fire that night.

As his family grew up and married, he became known as "Grandpa Billy" Kane. Having taught his own sons to ride, hunt, and ranch, he now enjoyed seeing his grandsons carry on the family traditions. At seventy-five, an age at which most men ride a rocking chair, he broke, with his gentle hand, a feisty young filly, and he continued to ride until he was nearly eighty-five. After that, Billy would saddle and bridle the mare, as he had always done, and they could be seen walking around the fields they knew so well, the horse obediently following the man. Undoubtedly they were remembering the good old days when a "little ride" started at sunup and ended at sunset.

Susan Watkinson Kane, born 24 August 1866, was tiny with dark, curly hair, and was considered a beauty. She was especially clever with her needle. Although only sixteen years old when she married, she made her own wedding dress of rust-coloured brocaded silk. The hand-made

Horse racing in Lillooet

buttonholes on this elegant dress are a work of art, a fact her granddaughter can attest to, for she has worn it on many special occasions. Because of her skill at sewing, Susan never discarded an article of clothing. Even clothes given to her for use in quilt-making were more often returned to the owner beautifully mended. Susan Kane washed, carded, and spun all the wool from their sheep, and when in later years she could no longer handle her spinning wheel, she continued to card and spin wool by hand onto a stick spindle. Although money was not a plentiful commodity, she kept her daughter beautifully dressed, and knit all the socks and sweaters for her husband and seven sons.

as with all pioneer families, the Kanes had their share of hard times, but there was always food for the table and a warm home to be proud of. Susan's greatest sorrow came with the burning of the log home that Billy had readied for her as a bride and where her children had been born and raised. All her treasures—family pictures and a fine collection of beautiful Indian baskets—were lost.

Susan Kane died in 1943 and was buried in the private cemetery on the Kane ranch. Grandpa Billy died there ten years later.

Young Bill Kane no doubt wanted to emulate the renowned horsemanship of his father. He says that at about fourteen years of age, "I figured I was quite a cowboy and I chased and caught wild horses. I broke them to saddle and sold them for an average of $10 each; that was good money then." He also sold fox and coyote pelts for "side money" and being an excellent shot and an enthusiastic hunter, added to his extra money by selling "buck deer" meat at eight cents a pound, clearing about twelve dollars per animal. The urge to be successful led him later to dabble in stocks, to his father's chagrin. When he wanted to buy Boeing Aircraft shares at forty cents, his father advised against it. "They'll never be able to fly by machine," he insisted.

Young Bill also got "mining fever" as a young man and staked on two good locations. Twice he found buyers, but his partners could not bear to part with the claims for the offered price, and dreams of a fortune blew away like the morning mists on his benchland home. On his own, he staked a "placer lease" and got some nuggets which were worth three dollars each, but after mining for five years, he decided to continue farming.

In 1960 he sold both his ranch and his father's estate, retaining for himself and his wife Annie four of the 720 acres he once farmed. From Kane's Acres, as he calls his small spread, he can still look out over the land, now all under cultivation and dotted with fine cattle, on which he has lived all his life.

Joseph Haller of Big Bar

Joseph Haller, long known and respected in the Lillooet-Lower Cariboo area, was born in Pittsburgh, Pennsylvania in 1825. He left home early in 1858 and went to the gold mines in Sacramento, California. Here he heard of the gold rush in the Colony of British Columbia, and he came by ship to Victoria.

Joseph Haller of Big Bar Creek

His son Edward James Haller said of his father, "My father owned and ran the first licensed house in the interior, selling liquor at his trading post. He traded with miners and Indians, selling tools, clothes, etc., and giving credit to the miners. That was at Big Bar Creek, where he lived about a couple of years. He was a packer for the miners, going to Quesnel and all over the place. He is supposed to have carried the mail from Yale to Lillooet, twice a year, for which he received $5 a letter. He packed it on his back, or on horse, however they could best get across the river. The young men used to value their sweethearts' letters pretty highly then!

"My Dad packed all through the gold rush, from 1858 to 1866. Then he pre-empted his land on Big Bar Creek, after he gave up the packing.

"He built a home of hewn logs and a small sawmill, making all the machinery himself, save the saw which he bought. He erected a grist mill and ground wheat into flour and cracked wheat, and in his blacksmith shop he made wagons and sleighs. On a farm of 160 acres he grew hay and vegetables, and bred saddle horses and cattle.

"He had nine children; seven boys and two daughters....

300 yards away from his shack. He did the best he could to save them, but so many died; he dug a big trench and buried them there in their blankets. He managed to pull through two of them, one man and one woman; the Indian woman eventually married a German named Conrad Kostering, who lived down the river, and they had a family.

"Indians? Yes, there were lots of Indians there. I used to play with the Indian children, and knew lots of them well. I used to be able to talk Shuswap quite well. Many of the Indians were very pleasant and trustworthy.

"One story I remember hearing: one late spring three pack trains amalgamated together. The horses were pretty thin at that time of year for want of food. They started on a trip and the Indians followed them. Then they started to climb the mountain at Naas River and it started raining and snowing, so the men and the horses got all played out. The head packers offered the men the

Packhorses photographed near Lillooet

A.W.A. Phair photograph

"He died at Big Bar Creek in 1900, living there all the time after pre-empting the land. He always had a free house there; everybody was welcome. You could just go right in—no pantries or fridges in those days. He was a prospector before he took up packing; he was a good prospector. He was religious, which is always a good thing.

"In 1861 the Indians had smallpox up at Big Bar Creek, right near my Dad's camp, about 200 or

goods if they would stop there and trade with the Indians, but the workmen would not, as they said that the Indians would kill them and take the goods anyway. They were worn out, and all their clothes were worn out, too. They dumped the goods on the ground and emptied the sacks of flour and took the bags to use for clothing to get back in—I suppose to Lillooet. They left all the goods right there in the swamp, on the mountain.

There was one old Indian lady there, she saw the flour lying on the ground and ran up and scooped it up in her skirt; when she went to stand up the string on her skirt broke and the flour went all over everything—moccasins and all! The boys had a great laugh. They even had to kill off some of the horses which could not make the journey back. It cost the packers thousands of dollars. The Indians were so hungry that they mixed up this loose flour straight away into a dough, wound it round a stick, and started eating it before it was half cooked. The Indians knew what beans and coffee were, but had not seen peas before; they picked them up, looked at them and then threw them away....

"I went to school at Big Bar; was there for two and a half years. It was not much of a school, and I did not get much book education, but I got lots of practical education years later, working with the Public Works. I was with the Public Works from 19 until I retired and came to live in Vancouver in 1942."

☆ ☆ ☆

Following are excerpts from letters translated from German which Mr. Joseph Haller wrote during 1858-1860 to his family in Pittsburgh. The salutations were all the same: "Dear Mother, Brothers and Sisters."

Sacramento, California.
June 7th, 1858.

...I will be on the Fraser River on 4th July, and probably digging gold. The territory belongs to England. I shall sail on 9th or 10th June from San Francisco to the Frazer River on the steamer "Panama." I paid $32 for the fare.

Somewhere on the Frazer River.
September 5th, 1858.

I have arrived on the Frazer River and I am making from $8 to $10 per day. I am in the best of health and thank God for it. The journey lasted 57 days.

Food is very dear, one pound flour $1.50, pork $1.75 per lb., beef $1.00 lb., sugar $1.50, beans $1.45, 1 lb. tobacco $6.00. Everything is dear but we hope that it will get cheaper. I would like to send $100 to you, but it is impossible; I am too far in the mountains, it will cost me more than $50.00 to send it and I would not be sure if you got it or not. I am anxious to hear from you, as I have not yet had a letter....

Cameron Bar, Frazer River.
May 7th, 1859.

...I am still on the Frazer River and intend to stay here during the summer. I earn from $5 to $6 a day. I have saved $700 so far. It is impossible to send money because it would cost me $100 to go to the next station, and I would have to risk my life....

Camerons Bar, Frazer River.
May 18th, 1859.

...I am still well and am making from $5 to $6 a day. I haven't got as good a claim as some on the river. I believe it will last me two summers. The food is not as dear now as last fall; we bought flour this spring for 28c per lb. So everything is cheaper than last year.

Victoria.
December 10th, 1859.

I take up my pen to write to you to let you know where I am. I am in Victoria, V.I. I shall probably stay here until February, then I am going back on the river to the gold mines. I came over here mostly on account of my health. When you are out on the river you haven't got anything to eat but bread, beans and pork. Last winter we were all in sick with swollen legs and rheumatics.

It cost me $100 to get here. When I go back again I will take my grub with me as that will be a lot cheaper than buying it there if I am lucky. I am healthy so far and hope you are the same, as I see in your last letter you are well and I was certainly glad to hear it. Everything is cheaper here on Vancouver Island; potatoes 1½c, flour $6 to $12 a barrel, onions 8c, beef 20c, pork 25c. Sugar, tea and coffee are cheap too. Tobacco is 50c per lb., schnaps $1 to $8 a gallon, board by the week $7 to $10, one drink of schnaps 12½c. Clothes are also cheap. When you write, write to Cameron Bar as before, for I won't stay here long. Best regards to all my friends. I hope that you are doing fine and don't forget me. Write as soon as possible.

Victoria.
February 9th, 1860.

I take up my pen to write a few lines. I shall go up the river again. I leave Victoria the 11th or 12th of this month for the gold mines at Camerons Bar, Frazer River. I am well and hope you are the same. I am going up the river with five men in a canoe which carries five tons. We bought all our food in Victoria because it is a lot cheaper than we can buy it up there. We take everything with us. It costs me $150 for my share. The winter was very mild in Victoria; we had snow only once in Victoria. There are about 5,000 men and 800 women, not counting Indians....

Lillooet shopkeepers in an era of more stable prices than those quoted by Joseph Haller—the early 1900s.

Victoria, B.C.
December 23rd, 1860.

...In March I bought twelve donkeys. I paid $2,300; I had to take a loan of $1,600. I am out of debt now and have $600 coming, only I cannot get it before March next year. I have got no money, I even have to borrow some to buy grub to get back to the river; I can get as much as I want for 2 per cent interest per month.

I should leave around 1st February for the river again. I am going to Lillooet, to Alexander and to the Forks of Quesnel River; from Lillooet to Alexander it is 220 miles, from Alexander to Quesnel is 60 miles. I am going to pack there with the donkeys; it pays fairly well, only it is very cold up there in Alexander. There is 4 to 5 feet of snow; at Lillooet there is not so much, not more than 6″ to 10″ snow. There are big mountains and the snow stays on them all summer. On the road from Lillooet to Alexander to Quesnel River it is very cold when it is raining. Last summer I had half an inch of ice in a bucket of water. On 20th July, the last time I came down, I was riding through snow. I left up there on 1st November and was in Lillooet on 6th November. The grub in Lillooet is a bit cheaper than it was before. Flour is $14 barrel, potatoes 6c per lb., beef 20c to 25c per lb., pork 40c to 45c per lb., tea 80c per lb., coffee 32c, sugar 25c. So everything is a lot cheaper than it was before. The prices given are what I gave in Lillooet....

Lillooet, B.C.
February (?) 17th, 1862.

I take up my pen to write you a few lines on how everything is going on here. I am all right so far. It was a hard winter and very cold. I had bad luck, twelve of my jackasses croaked last winter. I will start to work again soon. There are many people coming to this district now and I believe they will all make good this year. The grub is very dear again, flour $30 per 100 lbs. There is too much snow yet to do any freighting, so no grub is coming in. Donkeys are very dear right now, from $300 to $400 apiece, horses $150 to $250 apiece, and beef 25c per lb. on the hoof. I am tied up very short this time. I am hoping for an answer.

Lillooet, B.C.
April, 1862.

...It was a very hard winter, we had 24 to 30 inches of snow. And it was very cold, 34° below zero. They have opened a few new mines around here, and they claim they are good. I hope that they are good so that business will pick up for me, and for everyone else in this country.

My donkeys are all in good shape. If I do well this summer I will try to come home this Fall if I can find somebody to take care of my donkeys until I come back. It would be nice for me if I could see you all once again. It is more than eight years since I left home. I shall go back to the gold mines to my old business, packing, this summer. I have got sixteen donkeys and a horse now, and there are not many better donkeys for packing in this country than mine. They carry from 300 to 400 pounds each, ten to twenty miles each day all summer long and stay fat in spite of everything....

I have not been hungry a single day that I've been in this country. But there are a lot who do go to bed hungry, that is if they have a bed. Most of them carry a bed on their backs wherever they go. The bed is nothing but one or two blankets....

Lillooet.
September 18th, 1862.

...I had good luck so far this summer, only I lost one donkey three days ago; he broke a leg and I had to shoot him. My business is going pretty good. I bought six more donkeys for $200 apiece. I now have twelve donkeys and one horse, and a house on the road to the gold mines. It pays pretty well so far, and I hope to do still better in a month's time because all the miners are coming down to Lillooet and Victoria. Grub was very dear again this year but now it is a little cheaper. Flour $14 per hundred pounds, pork 37½c, beef 30c to 35c. So everything is a little cheaper this year. My house is 55 miles from Lillooet, up the Frazer River. I have got 6 tons of grub in the house now and I am taking another three tons up, because I can sell everything during the winter and make a little profit. You can't get anything up there in winter without having it packed in by Indians, and that is too dear. I close my letter in the best of health and hope you are the same.

Lillooet.
November 5th, 1862.

...I am 55 miles up the river from Lillooet. I have got a house for the travellers and a store with grub. [Haller also had a saloon, which was known to the miners as "The Red Dog Saloon."] I have 8,000 lbs. of flour, 600 lbs. pork, 90 gallons schnaps of different kinds. I have got $8,000 to $9,000 of grub and all kinds of clothes for the winter. My house is on Big Bar Creek, Frazer River, B.C. The picture shows you the house and surroundings. My donkeys are all fat this fall. I have got twelve now, and one horse. I lost one donkey, no bad luck with them this year. Flour is worth $25 to $26 per barrel, pork 37c to 40c per pound, sugar 25c to 30c per pound; in my store flour is $25 to $30 per hundred pounds. I have got about 5 thousand dollars debts now but the grub will pay everything and a lot more when all is sold. By the spring I won't have much left. When I sell my flour I guess I will be out of debt, this will be about April.

Big Bar Creek.
December 31st, 1862.

...I hear every day that the war is not over yet. I have got a house on Big Bar Creek and a good stack of groceries. I have got 3 tons of flour, 1,000 lbs. beans, coffee, sugar, butter and everything in the line of grub, and all kinds of clothes, and tobacco and whiskey; 7 head of cattle, 3 steers, 9 sheep and a chicken house. My house is more a restaurant; it belongs to me and a friend of mine. I have got 13 donkeys and a horse of my own that do not belong to him. The donkeys and horses are very dear this year, because too many died last summer. Donkeys are $200 to $300 per head, horses $125 to $200 per head. Flour is 25c to 28c per pound, tobacco is $3 a pound, beef 25c to 30c a pound, pork 50c to 70c per pound. The cattle cost me $100 each, the sheep $21 each. In a distance of about one mile around

Lillooet in the early 1900s

are sixty to seventy Indians; they are very nice and do not harm the white people.

Big Bar Creek.
December 27th, 1863.

...It is a very mild winter so far. We have not had any snow yet and the water is low in the river. I have got ten donkeys and a horse. I did not lose one this summer and hope I won't lose any this winter. They are all in good condition so they can stand the winter.

The grub is very dear through all the Cariboo; flour is 45c to 50c a lb., pork $1.00 to $1.25 a lb., tobacco $3.00 to $4.00 a lb., beef 40c to 50c a lb. Everything is cheap for this place. The gold is deep but there is plenty there. When they get it they strike it rich. I know men who have made $100 to $1,000 a day once they have struck it. But a poor man can't do a thing here. A common man gets $10 a day when he knows his job. I have got a claim in Cariboo but I don't know yet if it is good or not.

Lillooet.
April 25th, 1864.

...I am healthy and feeling fine and I am starting to pack again. Business is very bad and there is not much work. I believe it will be better in about two months. The groceries are cheap here, and in Williams Creek the flour is 40c to 45c per pound; pork $1.25 to $1.50 a pound, tobacco $3.50 to $4.00 a pound, sugar $1.25 a pound, beef 35c a pound. We had a mild winter so far. I am closing my letter in the best of health and hope you are the same....

Lillooet Flat.
October 16th, 1864.

...I am still in Lillooet, and tomorrow I shall go to Big Bar Creek again where my house is, and I shall stay there until spring. I am healthy and feeling fine so far, and I thank God for it. Times are very bad this year, I made nothing during the summer....

Big Bar Creek.
December 26th, 1865.

...We got plenty of snow this Fall; if it stays all winter it is possible that many horses and donkeys will die. I have twelve donkeys and a horse, and all are in good shape for the winter.

I shot a deer, the four quarters weighed 206 lbs. It was a big fellow, the biggest that was shot around here. I have shot big ones before but not as big as this one....

Quesnelle Mouth.
July 8, 1866.

...I spent the last winter in the best of health that I have ever been in. If I had nothing to do I would go out hunting for fresh meat and I would have pretty good luck. I got five deer and sold some of the meat for 15c per pound.

Business is not very good. Grub is fairly cheap, flour is $17 to $20 a hundred pounds, pork 50c to 62½c a pound, sugar 33c to 40c a pound and beef 15c to 30c a pound....

Cameron Bar.
August 24th, 1866.

...It is impossible for me to send money because I bought twelve donkeys for 200 dollars apiece, so that means $2,400. I had to take up a loan, on which I have to pay 3 per cent interest per month. I hope I can send $200 to $300 in two or three months when I am able to work. The man who mails the letter is a partner of mine; he was my partner at Cameron bar, his name is J. Dartan. I am making pretty well with the donkeys....

Mr. A.M. Beck   *Big Bar Creek.*
                                 April 11th, 1890.

My dear Nephew:
With great pleasure I again will drop a few lines to you, hoping sincerely you are as well as ever.

We are all quite well now but two weeks ago we were all very sick for 3 or 4 days. I am not quite well myself yet, but the others are over with their colds.

Our Spring is not quite opened yet, we are still having snow, and pretty cold days, but still it's neither sleighing nor wheeling from here to Clinton on account of the snow being too deep. The express man goes on horseback now. I think this is a very backward spring we are having this year.

Dear Nephew, little Gust received the nice suit of clothes you sent him. I tell you he was very much pleased with them; we asked him what he would say to you for them, he says many thanks to you for them; also accept our best of thanks for your kindness.

Tell Mary we received also the handkerchiefs she so kindly sent to us, and many many thanks to her for her fond remembrance of us.

Your Tyee is wanting you to come out again and help him to hunt geese, duck and swans; he is busy hunting every spare time he gets, he is the best hunter we have here.

There are any amount of deer in bands in the horse pasture; there are going to be plenty of deer. So when you come you will be able to kill some, by the dozen.

Your Punch (Tyee) has broke(n) his Pony, Brandy, in harness, he was very gentle and acted like an old horse.

I guess all the farmers down at Big Bar have finished putting in their crops. All the folks around here are enjoying good health that you know, excepting we heard two days ago Mosi Pigeon was very sick, he may be getting better again.

I will end my letter for this time with the kind love of all, hoping to hear from you again, and that soon.

We had an increase in our family on the 28th March and he was baptized this morning by Revd. Father Marchall; his name is Edward James Haller, he is getting on very fine so far. Gust is very fond of him, he calls the baby a bawl baby when he cries.

Write to us soon again.

Your affectionate Uncle,
Joseph Haller

Ranches on the Lillooet-Pavilion Road

Chief Sam Mitchell, Fountain rancherie, provided the following information:

MILE 0: Parsonville, across the river from Lillooet, was designated Mile 0. It was from here that Sgt. Major John McMurphy and his group started in May 1862 and erected mile marks as the work progressed. They first followed a part of the road built by G.B. Wright.

15 MILE ranch was started by a Bill Keithley. He died and his widow ran the ranch alone until she married a teamster by the name of Foster.

17 MILE ranch was owned by the widow of Clarke Ballewd (not to be confused with his father, the well-known Bun Ballewd). This was originally the Bailey ranch.

18 MILE ranch was originally owned by Tom Cole, the uncle of Dan Hurley. The old house has been torn down.

19 MILE ranch was first owned by O'Halloran, an Irish Catholic who brought his wife out from Ireland. They had a daughter who became a nun, and a son, Cornelius O'Halloran, who was a judge in Victoria. Mr. O'Halloran, Sr., died in St. Paul's Hospital, Vancouver.

18 MILE and 19 MILE ranches were bought by a Mr. Tiffin, a wealthy Vancouver man who combined them into one ranch.

20 MILE ranch was owned by Phil Garrigan, an American, who built the ranch and a store. He had a very good business and his son Pete Garrigan drove a freight wagon for the store. Both father and son were good blacksmiths.

Between 20 Mile and 21 Mile (between Garrigan's and the flour mill) was a place owned by a Mr. Hugh.

21 MILE, where the Pavilion Hotel and store are now, was a flour mill built by a Mr. Lee and operated as late as 1909. The wheat came from farmland at Sky Lake and some was grown on the west side of the Fraser, very high on the benches. It was brought down by 20 pack horses, unloaded, loaded onto a ferry operated by a Mr. Maddison, taken across the Fraser where another 20-horse pack train took it uphill to Cumming's (or Lee's) mill.

PAVILION RANCHERIE is on the Fountain reservation. A rancherie is an Indian village, and Pavilion Rancherie has an Indian name, "Squilah" (pronounced Squeela), meaning "Frosty Ground." With Fountain Mountain rising behind (southside), this area does not have sun for too long during the winter days.

FOUNTAIN RANCHERIE: The Fountain Indian Band now live at what was the old Fountain Ranch. This ranch received its name from a mountain spring which comes out like a fountain and is now right behind Chief Sam Mitchell's house. This ranch was first started by a man named Lorenzo Latero. Nicholas Colenda took over from Lorenzo, and after a survey this ranch contained all but the north forty acres, which were Indian land. Colenda ranched the Fountain until he died, when he willed this fine piece of land to Mrs. Paul Santine (nee Josephine Odine). She and her husband, who had had a store in Lillooet, ranched here until 1914 when a Mr. McKinnon from Vancouver bought the ranch. During World War II some Japanese bought the Fountain Ranch, using the name Nels Jergensen. They grew tomatoes and had good crops for six or seven years. After 1945 the Japanese went back to the coast. In 1952 the Indian Department bought the Fountain and combined it with the forty-acre piece for the present Fountain Reservation.

The Bryson family at The Grange

The Bryson Place

Of the fine pioneer ranches that dot the Lillooet area, mention must be made of the Bryson Place.

John Bates Bryson, born in Nova Scotia in 1864, came to New Westminster in 1887, and in 1895 moved to Ashcroft where he and J.C. Smith operated a blacksmith shop. In 1899 the firm of Smith and Bryson bought the Grange ranch from Mrs. Martley. The men operated these two businesses jointly for two years; then Bryson took over the Grange and Smith retained the blacksmith shop.

John Bryson, realizing the potential of the area, looked about for more land to increase his holdings. The 350-acre Clark ranch on Pavilion Mountain was purchased by him, giving the Grange summer pasture on the mountain. A far-sighted rancher, Bryson planted timothy on the mountain meadows and fast-growing alfalfa on the lower ranch. By moving his thirty-five man team between the mountain and the flats, he was able to harvest three crops a season: alfalfa at the Grange, timothy at the higher level, and a second crop of alfalfa which was ready for cutting after the timothy was harvested. The hay was sold on the Cariboo Road, and the biggest chore was hauling it down the mountain in winter on sleighs. In addition to the ranch land, Bryson also owned shares in the coal company at Hat Creek.

When his ranch was in order, John Bryson courted Minnie Isabel Carson, daughter of Robert Carson, his neighbour on the mountain ranch, and they were married on 22 June 1904. Soon their home became a stagecoach stop; a room known as "the stage room" was set aside where meals were served to the passengers. The stage room was off-limits to the six Bryson children, but the rest of the house was reserved for the family, and their lives could continue uninterrupted while the guests were taken care of.

67

The Bryson family

John and Minnie Bryson had a daughter (Norma) and five sons (Robin, Norval, Clarence, Glen and Wildred "Duffy"). After their parents died in 1941 and 1942, the sons continued to run the family ranch. When it was finally sold in 1949, the boys had put such a ridiculously high price on it that they were sure their offer would not be accepted. But it was, and thus the Bryson Place, originally the Grange, passed out of the hands of the pioneer families associated with it.

CHAPTER
5

Chinese Around Lillooet

A.W.A. Phair photograph

Lillooet's China Town about 19[

L ittle has been written about the Chinese people who immigrated into British Columbia from California and from China.

Contrary to the belief that the Chinese mainly came for the building of the CPR, there was already a large Chinese population in the province during the early mining days. As early as 1858 they had come from San Francisco and from Hong Kong to follow the miners to Yale, often satisfied to glean the gold left in old mines which whites had left for richer claims. Three thousand Chinese were working the bars and "rocking for gold" in the late 1850s. As the lower fields became overcrowded, many Chinese headed for Barkerville, travelling the long distance on foot. Around the turn of the century, it was said, there were more Chinese than white people in Barkerville.

The early Chinese were looked upon as a source of cheap labour, and settlers would hire them to do hard work for much lower pay than a white would demand. No doubt they were often easy prey for smart businessmen. It was not generally understood that the Chinese hoped, by saving every penny they could make, to return to their homeland and their families in order to improve their living conditions. Many wanted to

Chinese men washing gold along the Fraser canyon

Provincial Archives, Victoria

groups was more profitable than working alone. Many of them made large amounts of money.

An early provincial law stated that a placer claim left unattended for more than twenty-four hours could be taken over, and the Chinese took advantage of this law. The whites' attitude towards the Chinese was well indicated in an article in the Victoria *Colonist* of 23 July 1859:

> The Chinamen in the Little Kanyon have occasional conflicts with white neighbours in which "John" is invariably wrong. The white men aver that the Celestials have pursued a most aggressive policy—jumping claims, while the owners were in town buying provisions; pulling up stakes and tearing down notices; and behaving in an insolent manner generally, thereby meriting a trouncing.

As most Chinese could not read, write, or speak English they often had to learn about the laws of the country through an interpreter who might create misunderstanding. They moved from one job to another, making it difficult for the whites to keep track of them. They often appeared similar and their names were difficult to pronounce. In the correct Chinese form the surname came first, and this caused confusion. Also, their names were often wrongly translated into English and many mixups occurred. In any legal situation requiring the setting down of a name, there was bound to be difficulty. Usually they were referred to as coolies, celestials, or the derogatory "John."

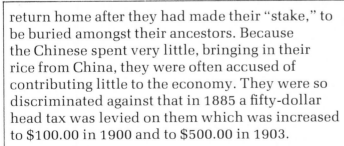

return home after they had made their "stake," to be buried amongst their ancestors. Because the Chinese spent very little, bringing in their rice from China, they were often accused of contributing little to the economy. They were so discriminated against that in 1885 a fifty-dollar head tax was levied on them which was increased to $100.00 in 1900 and to $500.00 in 1903.

The first Chinese miners around Lillooet worked the banks and bars of the Fraser, camping on the rugged shores wherever they could find a level spot. They spent rough hard winters with few comforts, little warmth and not much food. They huddled together in shacks and survived by sticking together. They learned that working in

Under these adverse circumstances, it is a marvel that many Chinese people were able to make a good living and to educate their families—a high priority for the Chinese people—and to become successful citizens of their adopted country.

The Chinese who lived in Lillooet were ranchers, miners and storekeepers. In pioneer days they usually wore their traditional working garb—loose coats without lapels, baggy trousers, black hats similar to the cowboys' cartwheel hats, and long queues.

Some of them smoked opium (their Joss House was situated where the present-day barbershop now stands), and they enjoyed a gambling game called Fa Choy. This was played by each holding out a hand with different number of fingers extended. The loser had to take a drink from a bottle of "Sam Suie" (which cost thirty-five cents a bottle), and the last man able to stand won the money.

The Chinese community had a Chinese herb doctor, Cee Hing Lung (or Long), whose patients included whites and Indians as well as Orientals. His son, Shung Cee Hing Lung, remained in the district and became a cook at the Bralorne Mines. Chung was also an herb doctor, who once, when he was being taken into Bralorne, asked his guides to shoot a bear for him. They were puzzled that he left the meat and took only the bear's feet, gall, and skin. Apparently these were used for his medicines.

Another chinese herb doctor, Ah Chow, demonstrated the healing properties of deer horn. A Mr. Windt had cut his foot with an axe, and as he was far from a doctor, attempted to cure himself, but the cut refused to heal. When Ah Chow was consulted he opened the cut and shaved minute particles from a deer horn into the wound; Windt's foot healed perfectly and caused him no more trouble.

Su Hing Ling was another typical Chinese immigrant who worked hard and lived frugally. He mined at Cayoosh Creek and later ran William Russel's ranch. When he grew old, he decided to return to China. Mr. Russel, who regarded Su highly, made the arrangements for him to get home. The government paid his passage to New Westminster, plus fifty cents taxi fare. He told Mr. Russel that he had "lotsa money home," and would live like a lord of the manor.

The first annual government mining report, 1896, describes the perseverance and ingenuity of

The Fraser River at Lillooet, B.C.

the Chinese miners. Many owned land on the banks of the Fraser between Lytton and Lillooet, as well as in the town of Lillooet. One entry shows that Ah Key, who was a British subject, owned a 160-acre Crown Grant of land fifteen miles below Lillooet on the west bank of the Fraser, as well as Lot 287 just below the 14 Mile Creek, now known as Lachore Creek. This parcel is listed today as Rosebank Ranch. On the Fraser's east bank, seven miles south of Lillooet, he received 160 additional acres on 19 October 1867. Ah Key's name is listed in the B.C. Settlers list, first in 1882-83 as a trader and then in 1891 as a farmer.

Another Chinese who owned land in the Lillooet district was Ah Chee, who took up a Crown Grant of ten acres on the east bank of the Fraser. The plot was known as Judge Elliott's Ranch and was almost directly across from Texas Creek.

Writer Norman Hacking tells the story of Kwan Loy, a miner in Lillooet for many years, who decided that the time had come to return to China, for he wanted to die in the land of his ancestors. He enquired into the fare to Vancouver, and found that he had to pay the stage fare from Lillooet to Lytton and the train fare from there. He decided that this was too much, and devised another means of travel to the coast. The day that he was ready to leave, he outfitted a rubber punt with a small stove, blankets, and his few possessions. Although his friends tried to dissuade him, he stepped blithely into his little boat and pushed it into the Fraser river. Word of his daring passed before him, and settlers along the river came to wave him on. When he arrived at Lytton, the alarmed populace shouted out, trying to stop him from attempting to go through Hell's Gate. Kwan Loy sat back placidly smoking his pipe, waving to those on shore. He made his tea and cooked his rice on his little stove, then rode through Hell's Gate and the other turbulent places on the river

Lillooet's commercial street in 1919, showing Wo Hing General Store to right

with no trouble at all, arriving at New Westminster in a record ten days. Here he unloaded his few personal belongings, kicked the punt out into the river, went to the interurban streetcar, and for thirty-five cents purchased a ticket to Vancouver. From there he embarked for his homeland.

another well-known Lillooet chinese was Wo Hing, who owned the China ranch on West Pavilion. He also owned a store in Lillooet where he sold the pork that he raised on the ranch. His well-cared for pigs were taken in summer to the range at the foot of a nearby mountain. Today its official name is Hog Mountain.

Wo Hing's store was one of Lillooet's larger establishments on the main street, and it backed onto an alley. Many Chinese families lived here, and it became known as China Alley. A Tong war once nearly broke out in the alley, but Dan Hurley, who was respected by the Chinese, persuaded the adversaries to give up their feud and return to their homes.

Chinese also mined and owned land at the Fountain on the Fraser. In the Upper Hat Creek district were two Chinese ranchers, "Old Duck," or "Joe Duck," whose real name was Tong Sing, and Mrs. Kwan Yip. Mrs. Yip's story is one of

courage and quiet determination to raise her family to be good citizens. She was very likely the first Chinese child born in Victoria. When her mother, Mrs. Lee Kwan, and two children came to Victoria from San Francisco in March 1860, the *Colonist* reported that "the appearance of the first Chinese woman to set foot in the Colony caused quite a stir." Lee Yee (Mrs. Kwan Yip) was born a year later.

The Kwans of Upper Hat Creek

Kwan Lee's story was told by her son, the late Arthur Kwan, who was born in Cache Creek and lived in Vancouver for sixty-nine years. The story he told of his family who pioneered in the Cache Creek-Upper Hat Creek areas is one of hard work, heartbreak and the determination of one small Chinese lady.

The first Kwan, Kwan Yip, came from Hong Kong as a young man on one of the old clipper ships, the journey to Victoria taking three months. He had heard stories of the goldfields and went first to Yale, where he worked on the rockers which at that time stood in rows almost covering the Yale Bar. They were operated by Chinese, Indians and whites.

Kwan Yip worked hard here, but it was frustrating work; the "flour" gold was sometimes so minute that it was impossible to gather. Eventually, the ingenious Chinese workers figured out a way to collect it. They shook the residue from the rockers into their bed blankets until the blankets were heavy with the combined sand and gold flakes. They then folded them many times, tied them firmly, and burned them in their campfire. When the ashes had cooled, the men sifted them for the gold, which had amalgamated into pieces that were easier to handle.

Kwan Yip moved to the Barkerville area from which came tales of tremendous strikes. He walked the entire distance, to discover the same story—a few hit "pay dirt," but most barely made wages, and some not even that.

Kwan and some other Chinese decided that a combined effort would be more lucrative. About twenty-five formed a small company so that they could manage bigger and better equipment and longer, larger sluice boxes. They worked for long hours, taking the skimmed milk from the rivers after the white men had taken the cream. Occasionally they made a good strike, but usually they just cleaned up the river after the white men had left their claims for richer fields. The Chinese were known to use brooms to sweep the last vestiges of the flour gold from the rocks and rills of the creeks.

Kwan Yip came back from the goldfields, and although he had not made his fortune, he had scanned the country well in his travels and had decided he would stay in this new land instead of returning to China. Cache Creek, with wagon roads fanning north, south and east, was a place that he fancied. There was water in the creek, grass in the bottomland, and grazing in the rolling hills. It was an attractive stopping place for travellers and a crossroads, so he started his store here.

In 1875, Kwan Yip journeyed to Victoria, where he married Lee Yee, who had been born there in 1861. He took his city bride back to the wilderness country of Cache Creek, and there they worked long, hard hours in his small business. It was a new and strange life for Yee, and she was often surprised by the kindness shown her by her white neighbours. In Arthur's words, "It was our white friends who trusted and helped my mother when she had no money to pay; the Chinese were of the belief 'no money, no goods.'" This store was called the "Yee Yick Store," but it was given many other names such as "Yee Yip" and "Yip Yee," by non-Orientals who had difficulty with Chinese pronunciations. Situated in the centre of the meeting of the valleys, only a few miles from Ashcroft, the store specialized in groceries, but also carried a wide variety of goods, from needles and thread to lanterns. The wholesale suppliers, Kelly Douglas and Malkin, often traded goods for goods, with no money changing hands. Although the store never became a big, successful enterprise, with Yip and Yee working hard and each of their seven children pitching in as they grew old enough, it did keep a roof over their heads and food on the table. For twenty-six years the Kwans eked out a living at their Cache Creek store, until Kwan Yip died in 1901. He was buried at Cache Creek.

Left a widow with a family to raise, Mrs. Kwan continued to operate the store, but each year it became more difficult for her to make a living. She grew large crops of beans and potatoes, which she exchanged with the Vancouver suppliers for store goods. But her entire crop would net only about two tons of grocery supplies, and prices were so low that finally she had to give up the struggle and find another way to support her family.

Fortunately her neighbours rallied around her and lent her money, knowing that she would repay her debt when money was available. Each

child finished grade school and continued schooling whenever the family finances allowed.

With the help of a family friend, Joe Duck (Tong Sing), who had had a store next to them at Cache Creek, Mrs. Kwan learned of the Upper Hat Creek area. "Old Duck," as he was known to the ranchers, owned a large ranch there. He was a wealthy man, and ran 2,000 head of cattle. He also grew timothy and clover crops for feed. Kwan Yee, deciding that she could no longer make a living at the Cache Creek store, in 1907 moved her family to a homestead about five miles south of the Duck ranch and they proceeded to carve a home and ranch out of the wilderness.

Starting a homestead was a tremendous feat for a woman who had never ranched before. The land was about eighteen miles from the Hat Creek and Upper Hat Creek junction and was accessible only by horseback and wagon.

Not the least of Kwan Yee's problems was the requirement that she become a naturalized citizen before getting a Crown granted homestead, but she persevered and became a British subject in 1907. Because of the inability of officials to record Chinese names properly, she was naturalized as Annie Yee Yet. The Kwan homestead was known to local ranchers as the Yip ranch, from the name of the store in Cache Creek. The family remained here long enough to prove up on the homestead, and then Kwan Yee moved them to the Duck ranch.

Upper Hat Creek is not a large flow of water. It begins in an alpine-like meadow area, and twists and winds its way between the mountain ranges and through a narrow opening, following bottom-land of willows and swamp grass out to the valley of Hat Creek. Some say that the creek's name refers to the fact that a Hudson's Bay man lost his hat in the creek and had to leave it behind; others insist that the Indians named the creek for a large rock in it that resembled a hat.

At any rate, Kwan Yee enjoyed the beautiful saucer-like valley, with its meadow flats rolling up to timber line and then the granite tops of the mountains rising above the trees. The old road over which Yee travelled followed the creek bed along the floor of the valley. Everywhere there was something of interest to observe. There were alkali-rimmed ponds, cacti on the hills, thunder eggs and other evidence of former volcanic activity. The rolling grass hills were fenced and cross-fenced with poles; the lower hay meadows were patched with willows and golden poplars. Kwan Yee learned to love the beautiful summer days and crystal-clear nights and to endure the cold, windy winters when the temperatures could drop to fifty degrees below zero.

Kwan Yee had nine children in all, seven born to Kwan Yip and two to Joe Duck. Eventually four of the children, Ernie, Jack, Arthur, and May, returned to the homestead and operated the ranch themselves. They ran 600 head of cattle, on one occasion driving 100 head as far north as Hazelton. The Kwan boys were good cowboys and looked after their cattle well. They fed them through the winter months when other ranchers were letting their animals forage or eat hay from a stack, and in February when meat was in short supply in the Lower Mainland, they were the only ones to have cattle to sell.

In 1912, Kwan Yee became ill. Arthur took her to the hospital in Vancouver, where it was discovered that she had tuberculosis. She died the following year. Arthur stayed in Vancouver and took over the responsibility of looking after the two Duck children whom he had brought with him from Hat Creek. He knew how important education had been to his mother, so he worked in order to be able to send them to school.

Eventually, Ernie, Jack, and May also left the ranch and moved to Vancouver, and some time later, the Kwan spread was sold to a young man named Henry Parks.

CHAPTER
6

Neighbouring Lytton: The Hautiers

Three Mile Canyon, three miles above Yale on the Fraser

Because of Lytton's location where the Fraser and Thompson rivers meet, the town played an important part in the history of Lillooet. The Fraser River was the means by which freight was transported before the railway was built in the 1880s, and the Lytton trail was a major access route to Lillooet, culminating in the present roadway which was completed at the turn of the century.

Originally referred to as Camchin, which was the name of the Indian village across the river, the town was formally named Lytton on November 11, 1858, by Sir James Douglas "as a mark of respect and a merited compliment for Sir Edward Bulwer-Lytton, Secretary of State for the Colonies, a representative of Her Majesty, Queen Victoria."

Thousands of dollars in gold passed through the settlement on its way to Victoria; thousands of miners and railroad workers converged on the town during the gold rush and railway building activity. Many of the pioneers who arrived here were just passing through, but one who stayed, captivated by the breathtaking beauty of the setting—valleys cleaved by the winding ribbons of the rivers; granite mountains towering over forested countryside—was Louis Hautier.

A young Belgian, he arrived in San Francisco in 1858 and upon learning of the Cariboo strikes, travelled north to Victoria. Here Hautier left his family and proceeded to seek his fortune. He made the trek north from Yale on foot and when he reached the future site of Lytton he stood on the banks above the Great Forks looking over the expanse of country and declared, "This is where I will build my hotel. It is the joining of two rivers and one day there will be a town here."

Louis Vincent Hautier

carried Alphonse in a basket on her back. The way over the mountain was hazardous, but it was not to be compared with the perils encountered in parts of the canyon. Lasha carried both children through the canyon. She was a devout Catholic and would never venture with the children onto the floating bridges—strings of logs tied end to end crossing the surging waters—until she had made the sign of the Cross.

"Lasha" with friend pointing to camera

So Louis Hautier turned from his dream of finding a gold mine to the more practical plan of building a hotel. He already knew from experience that future travellers would be footsore after making their way from Port Yale to Spuzzum and that they would find only frustration when they tried to cross the turbulent waters of the Fraser and discovered the sheer rock walls along the river. He also knew that in order to bypass the turbulence of Hell's Gate, they would be forced to climb over Jackass Mountain and down to the benches on the west side of the river before they found rest. Hautier intended to provide them with a place to rest. Thus it was that the Globe hotel became the first stopping place north of Yale on the Fraser River.

It was 1860 before Hautier's hotel was built and he was sufficiently established to bring his wife, daughter and new son, Alphonse, born in Victoria on 2 September 1859, to their new home. The journey was an unforgettable and frightening experience for Josephine Hautier, who was used to city life and to the gentler terrain of her native Belgium. The vastness of British Columbia and its mountains overwhelmed her. After the family disembarked from the steamer which had brought them as far as Yale, they made the rest of the trip on foot. Eight Indian packers carried their belongings, and an Indian woman named Lasha

On 9 July 1862, an advertisement appeared in the New Westminster *Columbian*:

L. Hautier & Co's Hotel
★★★Billiard Saloon★★★
Lytton City, B.C.

This house is furnished in the best style and a stock of excellent liquors and cigars kept constantly on hand. The billiard tables are unsurpassed in the Colony. The charges moderate. Good stabling and horses constantly on sale at low prices.

The hotel earned the reputation of offering the best meals and accommodation along the trail. Louis started a farm at Kanaka Bar, ensuring a steady supply of fresh vegetables, fruits and nuts for the dining tables. He planted alfalfa seeds that he had carried from California, and produced the first crop of alfalfa hay grown in B.C. From this he sold seed to others seeking to start ranches.

In addition to being a hotelier and a farmer, this young Belgian pioneer was an herb doctor,

79

and gained a reputation for curing children's ailments. Medical men and surgeons were few in the Colony, and Louis would travel many miles ministering to the sick while Josephine looked after the hotel business. Hautier's medicines consisted of herbs, bark and roots of mullein, Oregon grape and other plants which he gathered in the hills. He boiled and stewed them on the kitchen stove, concocting secret remedies that had amazing results.

he also gained some fame for his surgical skills, particularly in removing corns. Once, when he was in Victoria, he was called to see Sir James Douglas, who had remarked to a friend, "I would give a great deal to be relieved of my corns...." The friend contacted Hautier, and on examination Louis discovered that the governor had five particularly bad corns, which he agreed to remove for the sum of five dollars each. Douglas thought the price too high and offered to pay twenty dollars for the operation. Hautier accepted the money and performed the operation. When he next went to Victoria he was again called to see the governor. It seemed that one of the corns had reappeared. Sir James asked, "Did you not guarantee the corns would not return?" To which

Louis replied, "I did, but after I had done the job you only paid for four; so of course one grew again." The corn was again removed and Hautier collected the remaining five dollars and went on his way smiling.

Louis and Josephine Hautier lived in Lytton until they retired, and then moved to their ranch at Kanaka Bar. They had five children: Louise, Alphonse, Marie Mathilde, Lulu, and Albert. Their son Lulu drove stagecoach and freighter in the Cariboo and was a superintendent for the Wells Fargo Company in the Yukon, Alaska and the United States. Albert also drove stage coach and freight teams in the Cariboo, and assisted his brother Alphonse in running the hotel and ranch.

Alphonse, the best known member of this pioneer family, learned the hotel business from his father, and took over at Louis's retirement. When the Globe burned down, he rebuilt it and named it "The Lytton." His memories of the early days were vivid, and he loved to describe the old days to the entertainment of the hotel guests.

He remembered the building of the first Cariboo road through the canyon, which was completed in 1865, when he was six years old. He clearly remembered the advent of stagecoaches being pulled by six horses. He told stories of the twenty-yoke bull teams drawing large wooden freight wagons in tandem; a train of twenty beasts passing through Lytton led by wise old bell mares plodding up the steep grades of the road built on

Oxen on the Cariboo Road, 1897

Miller's Ferry crossing the Fraser at Lillooet

Some passed through the town with long faces of despair but were secretly carrying their gold to Yale…

the sides of "Fraser's" river; and the mule outfits, many of which came up from the Dalles in Oregon. He told stories of the camels brought to B.C. by Frank Laumeister, to be used for packing to the goldfields, and of the time two of these camels stopped overnight in Lytton. He described the tricks that the miners used to convey their gold from the diggings to the express office at Yale.

Some passed through the town with long faces of despair at going broke but were secretly carrying their gold to Yale in packs and furs. There were stories of miners being bushwhacked, cheated, even murdered; of holdups in which everyone was suspect. Alphonse loved to describe the "artillery-laden" greenhorns in their impractical garb, in sharp contrast to the old-timers with their heavy wool trousers, plaid shirts, and stout boots. He used to chuckle over the escapades of returning miners who had gone "outside" (to the coast) to enjoy the bright lights, or "had a bust" at Yale where there were dance hall girls, hurdy gurdy girls, a flowing supply of liquor—and poker games, where some lost their season's earnings and even chanced their rich claims on the turn of a card.

He painted a vivid picture of the gamblers, those dandies with fine clothes and sleek hair. And he usually ended his story-telling with the recollection that "in those days the river banks were crowded with miners of all nationalities. Meals cost a dollar a plate; beds, wooden beds with straw mattresses, a dollar-fifty a night, or fifty cents to spread your blankets on the floor. Drinks were twenty-five cents. There was no money in circulation. Everything was paid for with gold. Plenty work, plenty to eat and drink, and always a dollar in your pocket. That is more than I can say now for some of them, but never mind, the good old times are coming back some time."

To those who wintered at the Hautiers' hostelry, Alphonse was a generous host. Many of the guests enjoyed their stay and went on their way without paying. The good-natured hotel-keeper trusted them to send out their money when they made their strike. It is told that he once fed eighteen men for a winter while hiring a staff of twelve to run the hotel.

He was also in great demand as a fiddler, and was seldom absent from the dances held up and down the Cariboo Road. Sometimes he would travel overland to Savona, at the west end of Kamloops Lake, and then go by sailboat to Kamloops. He played throughout the Nicola valley and as far north as Barkerville. Of those days he said, "You bet I made those girls and boys dance to my music."

Eventually Alphonse sold the hotel and bought land at Texas Creek halfway between Lytton and Lillooet on the south side of the river, where he started the Texas Creek Farm. He ingeniously rigged up a cable from the farm across the Fraser to the Lytton-Lillooet road. By sending a basket across on the cable, mail could be deposited in it by the mail carrier, and Alphonse would haul it back, saving himself a trip to Lillooet. Alphonse also prospected up the chines of Texas Creek and found high-grade molybdenum there. This he mined himself, but nearly "lost his shirt" by trying to pursue the enterprise on his own.

Louis and Josephine and three of their children are buried in the family cemetery at Kanaka Bar. The motto on their gravestone says it all: "Living they gave their best for the land they loved. Dying they remained a part of it."

CHAPTER

Old Lillooet Town

The place where Lillooet now stands was called Cayuse (pronounced Cayoosh) by the Indians who lived there. According to legend, some Indians were taking ponies, or "cayuses," up the creek which spills into the Fraser at this juncture, and the wild, unpredictable nature of the water so resembled their spirited ponies that they named the creek Cayuse, and the town as well. On 27 June 1861, while on a visit to the territorial outpost, His Excellency Governor Douglas changed the name to Lillooet.

Lillooet was an instant town that literally sprouted to accommodate the miners rushing north to the goldfields. The first government agent to reside in Lillooet was an Irishman, Thomas Elwyn, Justice of the Peace and Assistant Gold Commissioner, who was appointed magistrate on 8 June 1959.

In 1863 the town had three hotels, owned by Messrs. Herkimer, Nelson, and Boyle respectively. The *British Colonist* reported that "they are commodious and well furnished affording comfort to their patrons," and "the proprietors deserve encouragement as they have invested a good deal of capital in their establishments." These hotels were situated on the main street and served miners, packers, government officials, and

Excelsior Hotel, 1 July 1919

☆ ☆ ☆ Lillooet Brewery ☆ ☆ ☆

Jacob Meltz, proprietor, has always on hand a large and superior stock of Lager Beer; at the bar will be found the best of brandies, wines, segars; the public are invited to call. Prepared to fill orders promptly.

As well as the brewery and hotels there were a number of saloons and a bowling alley.

The first stores were log cabins fitted with shelves and supplied with merchandise brought in by the packers. When miners came down from the north to stock up on supplies, goods sometimes ran short, but generally they were filled with merchandise of all kinds and in large quantities, and goods were always sold in liberal terms and at fair rates. Soon these log cabins were replaced with wooden frame buildings, and by 1863 the directory listed eleven merchants in Lillooet.

all who came by. Food was plentiful but plain, and the owners were generally paid in gold dust.

While the hotels provided comfort for the travellers, an enterprising fellow named Jacob Meltz catered to their thirsts. In 1861 he built a small but well designed brewery for the manufacturing of lager beer. The *Colonist* of 12 January 1863 reported that Meltz had a large trade, "both with the upper country and for local consumption....The article is not inferior, we understand to any imported, and, on the principle of supporting home manufacture, deserves encouragement. A good deal of the barley is grown on farms in the neighborhood." Jacob Meltz advertised his establishment in the *Cariboo Journal*:

St. Mary the Virgin church

St. Mary the Virgin, an Anglican church, was the first to be built in Lillooet; it was consecrated 12 September 1862. Situated on a picturesque site adjoining the town, it was a beautiful little church had a parsonage and an excellent resident rector in the person of R.C. Lundin Brown, A.M. The church is now the site of the Lillooet Museum. Later, Catholic priests opened an Oblate mission on Seton Lake near the present town of Shalalth, and not long after, a Methodist church was erected in Lillooet.

The mining booms of 1858, 1862, and later drew many people of varied backgrounds to Lillooet; as well as miners, the town attracted professional men, government representatives and businessmen. Typical of those was Joe Watkinson, pioneer miner, rancher, and operator of a stopping place. He came to Yale in the late 1850s to mine. In 1860 he came north with eight other men to Lytton and travelled over Fountain Mountain. The men spent a year building a flume ditch to the flats at Parsonville on the banks of the Fraser opposite Lillooet in order to bring water down the hillside for a mining operation. The remains of this flume can still be seen near the Lillooet-Pavilion road.

In 1865, Watkinson settled on the 24 Mile ranch on a bench above the river, where he farmed until his death in 1914. Joe was an astute fellow who worked his place into a paying venture. His produce was shipped down the river to Lytton, a fast trip with the current helping. Of course, the trip back was another story, and there are still traces of the trail used by "pullers" on the river bank. In some places, mules or horses were attached to lines which hauled the boat against the current; in other areas, Chinese were hired to pull the lines.

Watkinson's ranch became a well-known stop for freight wagons and stages en route between Lillooet and Lytton. Here the stages changed horses and the passengers stopped for a home-cooked meal. Watkinson's Bar (now known as Foster's Bar), on the river below the ranch, was a whistle stop for the boat. Joe also mined this bar and got a few good pokes of gold for his efforts.

The first doctor in Lillooet was Dr. Henry Featherstone, an Englishman. His small office and log cabin stood on a site behind the present-day post office. When patients needed prolonged attention, he would often take them home and minister to their ills. An Indian housekeeper took care of his patients under his supervision. Outside of his professional field, Dr. Featherstone had a chequered career; he seemed to be before the courts frequently, either suing or being sued for one small matter after another. The 1863 Lillooet directory listed two other doctors: Dr. Gillingham and Dr. Alex Kennedy.

Flour was imported from Portland, Oregon, at $100 a bag, an astronomical price. A flour mill had been operating at Dog Creek since 1861, but the produce was sold only in the immediate area. Judge E.H. Saunders of Lillooet called a meeting and suggested that farmers grow their own wheat, thereby reducing the cost of flour. Judge Saunders promised free water and free land—300 feet in every direction—for a mill. A company was formed and the Lillooet Flour Mill was underway. The mill was built in 1864 on the east side of Cayoosh Creek, at a spot known as the Blue Pool. The mill used French burrstones and the machinery was made at the foundry of Sprat and Kriemler in Victoria. Its capacity was 10,000 pounds a day, and one season's produce was 300,000 pounds.

There was another mill operating in the area, Jonathan Hoeten Scott's mill at Parsonville. This was driven by steam power, the machinery from the steamer *Champion*, used on Seton Lake, having been purchased for this purpose. The three mills—Dog Creek, Lillooet Flour Mill, and Scott's Mill—were now able to meet most of the needs of the interior and little flour had to be imported.

These flour mills made a notable contribution to the economic life of the province. They made possible the development of agriculture by providing a market for locally grown grain, and they reduced the cost of living.

In 1868 the Scott mill closed and was moved to Clinton. The Lillooet mill continued to operate under the original management until 1881, when the property was sold to John A. Marshall, who had milled in many parts of the world. He came to Lillooet by way of mills in New Zealand, Oakland, California and Soda Creek, B.C. He ran the Lillooet for many years as Marshall's Mill.

Another miller was William Lee, who came into the area about 1864 and owned land near Rest Gulch, sixteen miles from Lillooet on the west bank of the Fraser. He started the Pavilion Mills in 1872, and "Water record No. 23 was issued at Victoria June 20th, 1872 to Pavilion Mill Co. for all the unappropriated water in Pavilion Creek and the lake at Marble Canyon." This diverted water was used to develop power to operate the flour mill. Lee was postmaster at Pavilion from 1884 to 1897, and was likely the first storekeeper there.

In 1863, Lillooet boasted a sawmill, owned by Messrs. Cadwallader and Company. This large mill contributed greatly to the town's prosperity by supplying lumber at a comparatively reasonable rate. The mill had a circular saw and an overhead wheel of large dimensions—very modern equipment for this remote town.

Agriculture was a successful business in the area, the light sandy soil with its gravelly subsoil producing crops equal to any produced in the finest soil in Canada. In addition to wheat and barley there were root crops such as turnips, carrots and potatoes which grew to an immense size. Indian corn was especially suited to the soil and climate, and a Mr. Letorra successfully grew grapes at Fountain from cuttings sent from his native Italy.

After the gold rushes subsided, the area became known as a big game hunting paradise. Many of the settlers became guides and owned large outfits of pack and saddle horses. Clients came from Europe, the eastern United States and Canada. Game was plentiful and varied, and hunting became an important new industry.

In 1859-60, Lillooet's population consisted of not more than thirty to forty white people and half a dozen houses. In 1863, there were "80 good buildings standing on a progress and a number not far from 100 inhabitants of fair skin." The 1863 directory of Lillooet gives a good idea of what services were offered to residents.

Coney	Supt. Govt. tolls
Connor	Packer
Guxor & Elmore	Merchants
Dodge, E.S.	
Edmondson & Co.	Butchers
Edwards	Merchant
Elliott, A.C.	& Postmaster
Farrel, J.	Merchant
Featherstone, H.	Drugstore
Foster, F.W.	Apothecary & Commission Merchant
Fellowes, Frank	Packer
Flynn	Ferry
Fritz	Tailor
Gillingham, C.F.	M.D.
Herkiner, J.	B.C. Stage
Hickson	Merchant
Hutchinson, Sr. & Jr.	Packers
Kennedy, Alex	M.D.
Lossack, G.	Constable
Mathieson & Crawford	Parsonville House
Mesereux & Miltz	Beer saloon
Nelson & Parsons	Merchants

Nelson, Charles	Restaurant
Newfelder	Merchant
Parker, J.	Saloon
Praeger	Merchant
Reed, R., Brown, B.A.	Merchants
Reed, J.R.	Deputy Sheriff
Sallise	Merchant
Towers & Thompson	Packers
Wallace	Blacksmith
Warden, C.	Merchant Packer
White, Fred	Packer
Wright, B.G. & Co.	Merchant

If the town of Lillooet was to attract desirable permanent residents, a school district was a necessity. The *British Columbia Gazette* of 22 October 1870 described the first school district as "all that piece of land included within a circle having a radius of three miles from the Court House." The first school was established in January 1873, and likely the first teacher was Miss Mary Jane Schubert, daughter of Augustus and Catherine Schubert, who had made the arduous journey with the Overlanders in 1862. Mary Jane Schubert received as her salary forty dollars per month, and the school that she taught in was "a single wooden building rented at $5.00 per month."

The following statistics were recorded in 1873:

School population between 5 and 16 years of age	22
Pupils between 5 and 16 attending school	19
Total number of pupils	19
Boys	14
Girls	5
Average attendance at school	13

Hillside view of Lillooet and Fraser River by A.W.A. Phair

Renee Chipman collection

87

Dan Hurley—
"Mr. Everything"

One man whose career embraced practically all the business activities in and around Lillooet was Daniel Hurley-Hadley.

Born in Truro, Nova Scotia, he arrived in Lillooet in 1865 when 18 years of age. He came to an uncle, Tom Cole, a well known rancher in the area.

Dan Hurley's son, Tom, with his mother

He started on his uncle's "18-Mile" ranch situated on the wagon road to Pavilion, and changed his hyphenated name to Hurley. At the end of two years, Tom Cole staked him to a stage-coach mail line operating between Lillooet and Clinton, and this turned out to be a successful venture for the young man. After he moved to Lillooet, Dan became a policeman and married Mary Mueller, daughter of Lillooet's first ferry operator. (The ferry was always referred to as Miller's Ferry, no doubt a simplification of Mueller's name.)

Dan was a tall, handsome man of aristocratic bearing, and having a keen business sense, he quickly became a leader of the community. At various times he owned a great deal of what is now Lillooet's Front Street, built the Victoria Hotel (now the Lillooet Hotel), owned a sawmill and a steamboat on Seton Lake, and had interests in three mines, the Lorne, Pioneer and Bend'Or.

Dan's interest in mining bore fruit when he was part owner in the Lorne Mine. One of the partners, John Williams, an experienced miner, had introduced the Arrastra mining method of crushing ore and the method was so successful that when the mine was sold, Dan Hurley's share was $37,000.

Hotel Victoria, 1919

Since the mine was in a remote area, the packing-in of supplies was a major job. The problems encountered are indicated by the story of moving fifteen head of cattle from the Carson ranch on Pavilion Mountain to the mine. The cattle were driven by Dan's son Tom down the mountain, into Lillooet, out Cayoosh Creek to Seton Lake. From there they were to be transported by barge to Shalalth, then driven over Mission Mountain, and finally up the Bridge River trail to the mine. When Tom got the cattle to Seton Lake, he found that the scow they were to be moved on had only rope railings. He questioned the operator, who assured him that everything would be all right. But as soon as the animals were loaded, they crowded to one side of the scow, and a number of them were soon in the lake. The men had quite a time retrieving the cattle from the water.

Once they brought twenty-five head from the Chilcotin, via Williams Lake, Clinton, Pavilion Mountain, Seton Lake, and up the trail. At the mine, two were butchered immediately and the rest taken to a corral in a meadow behind the mines. A week later, one of the men was sent to check on the animals, and found not a single head. A cattle posse traced the cattle tracks north to Gun Creek, over the Big Creek country, and back into the Chilcotin. The men—all cattle handlers—were amazed at this uncanny sense of direction in the animals, who had been brought to the Bridge River area by way of a completely different route, yet found their way back to their own home range by a more direct passage.

At the height of the mining activity, the town of Lillooet offered some relief from the hard work and remoteness of the mines when the miners came to town. Most men could afford the price of a good horse, and one of the big attractions was horse racing in the main streets. One July 1st there were 150 horses at the Lillooet Stampede.

There were also saloons and dance halls, and the old Victoria Hotel played an important part in the early days of the town. The miners, with a good poke of gold and raring for some fun, would more than likely come to the hotel and give their gold to Dan Hurley to hold. After a two- or three-day drunk, they would be refused more liquor, and Dan would tell them to sober up and hold on to some of their gold dust. The first time this happened to a man, he would invariably say, "Okay, if you won't serve me, I'll go to another hotel." Dan would always give the man his gold and away he would go, only to be back in a couple of days, broke and on his way to the mine. The next time, though, the man would come to Dan and ask, "Dan, how long can I stay drunk?" "Two days," Dan would reply. "All right, Dan, here's my money," the miner would say, and Dan would dole out the money so that it would last.

In 1904, Dan Hurley sold the Victoria Hotel, and that same year his uncle, Tom Cole, died. Dan went back to run the 18 Mile, adding 500 head of sheep to the 400 head of cattle already there. The 18 Mile was a good hay ranch, and in bad winters the ranchers from Upper Hat Creek would bring about 100 head of their cattle to Tom Cole to winter. Tom charged them five dollars a ton for hay in the stack. In the spring the ranch stock of cattle, pigs and sheep was taken to Barkerville for sale; the drive over Pavilion Mountain, out through Clinton, and up the wagon road to the mines was a gruelling trip. When Dan took over, he ran the ranch with the aid of Indian and white help. Indians were paid the going rate for ranch workers—one dollar a day; the whites, who were the top ranch hands, received one dollar and twenty-five cents a day. An example of prices during these ranching years is a sale of 87 head of cattle to Mr. Bryson for eighteen dollars a head; at the same time it is recorded that he was selling hindquarters of beef for eight cents a pound, three cents a pound for frontquarters.

Dan Hurley's knowledge of Lillooet was considerable, as illustrated by a story from town clerk Caspar Phair. One time Dan found a stranger starting to build on a vacant lot in the area and told him, "You are building on my property." The man did not believe him, and went into town to see the town clerk. When the stranger asked if Hurley owned the property, Caspar replied, "If Dan Hurley said it is so then it is. I have to go to him to find things out."

At the Big Horn ranch, Bridge River, 1911: Dan Hurley, centre; son Tom, far left

Caspar Phair came as a teacher to Lillooet and lived there for fifty-nine years, holding most of the government posts in town. He owned a store and took a keen interest in the mines and mining in the district. His son Artie was an excellent photographer, and it is to him that many of the early photographs depicting Lillooet must be credited.

When Dan served as a policeman under Caspar Phair he was so well respected that many suspects voluntarily came in who otherwise might have given trouble. Once Phair wanted a troublesome suspect brought in whom he knew was a friend of Hurley's. The suspect heard Dan coming and went out to meet him with a cocked rifle, calling, "Don't come any closer or I'll shoot." But when he saw it was Dan, he said, "Why did they have to send you? Okay, Dan, just let me get my things and I'll go with you—but not for anyone else."

An account in the Vancouver *Province* in 1936 by newspaperman George M. Murray tells how Dan celebrated the fiftieth anniversary of his arrival in Lillooet. Wrote Murray,

> By way of celebrating the 50th anniversary of his arrival in Lillooet, Dan Hurley, prospector and financier of Lillooet, made a journey by plane to Vancouver. He was a passenger with the well known Bridge River transportation man, Neal (Curly) Evans. The trip from Seton Lake took an hour and forty minutes.... In the last century Hurley has helped to extend the Lillooet trails. He gave his name to the Hurley River, a branch of the Bridge River, where there is much mining excitement.
> Once he fell down a shaft which he and other oldtimers had sunk at the Lorne. It was in midsummer, the heat unbearable and the flies very bad. With a broken leg he found it tough going on the saddlehorse which brought him back the 74 miles to Lillooet.
> But Dan survived that and is hale and hearty and optimistic at 68. And he lived to see the mine he helped start become one of the wonders of 1934.

Dan was still boosting his part of the country, as his words to Murray show:

> We grow the best cantaloupes, grapes, peaches and apples that British Columbia has ever seen. Our alfalfa seed is second to none. Our beef has the best flavor and texture of any in the interior. In other words, our ranching country is just about as valuable as our gold resources.
> Of course our Lillooet climate is equal to the best they have in California, bracing air and more sunlight than anywhere else in B.C., shorter winters and longer summers.

Mary Mueller, Dan's wife, was born and raised on the banks of the Fraser near the confluence of Cayoosh Creek on what is now the Rochard property. She was a beautiful young matron, apt to be mistaken as a sister to her eldest daughter. Seven children were born to the Hurleys—Susan Tudie, Minnie, Mabel, Ethel, Bernice (Babe), Tommy and Dan Jr. In 1904, the new home Dan completed for his growing family was the largest and most modern in Lillooet. It became the centre of Lillooet's social functions, for the Hurleys were an extremely hospitable couple and Mary was a gracious hostess.

Mary worked hard for the Catholic church, and Father Roher, the missionary who made Lillooet his home for more than thirty years, especially appreciated her hospitality. With her help, he was able to minister the needs of the Lillooet parish beyond the limitations of the church's finances.

When she died at age 86, the *Bridge River-Lillooet News* obituary written by the publisher and her friend Margaret Murray stated that she had lived "a long life of warm understanding, good neighborliness and exemplary motherhood."

Daniel Hurley died in Lillooet at age seventy-seven still believing that Lillooet would once more come into her own as the mining centre of the province.

John Scott, an Englishman, farmed land at East Lillooet later called Riverlands farm, and his grave, on the hill overlooking the mighty Fraser, is an historic site. On this farm he grew the famous "Lillooet bean," an excellent staple that is still in demand. He also grew some tobacco for sale.

Scott was a packer who had a large team of mules bringing from Yale the supplies sent on sternwheelers and steamboats from New Westminster. He packed flour, beans, coffee, tea, bacon, and miners' tools to the mine fields after the boats stopped freighting on Seton and Anderson Lakes. Scott's mule team was typical of pack trains of those times. The muleteers ("skinners" or "wranglers") packed the mules with sacks of flour, beans, etc., using just a blanket and ropes. At night the pack was untied and slid to the ground, if possible in the order that the mules were packed in the train. The mules were turned out to graze, and in the morning they were wrangled and each went straight to his own pack. The lead animal was called the Bell Mule and always carried the kitchen wares—dishes, pots, pans, and a half sack each of flour and beans. When the skinners were packing the mules in the morning they had to be very quick because as soon as the Bell Mule was packed she took off and the others followed, cinched or not. Sometimes a skinner had to run alongside a mule, cinching ropes as he ran, or else he would lose the load.

CHAPTER
8

Law and Order

Other than mining claim disputes and an occasional murder case brought in from outside the town, few cases were tried in the Lillooet court. Although the famous Hanging Tree is steeped in stories of hangings, old-timers say that they know of no actual case of anyone being hanged from its branches.

In such an isolated community, strangers stood out like sore thumbs, and if anything un-toward happened, the police usually knew where to look first. For a long time there was no jail in the town and suspects were allowed to roam the streets on their own recognizance. Apart from celebrating miners on a spree after months on their claims, Lillooet the town has been an orderly place.

The first magistrate to be appointed to keep law and order in this part of the colony was Thomas Elwyn. Although not much is known about his administration of justice, there is evidence that he was reprimanded for leaving his post without permission when he went north to investigate dubious mining practices.

Governor Douglas became aware that government officials were speculating in land and buying up tracts before they were advertised to the public. Miners began complaining that it was impossible to obtain justice while members of the judiciary were mixed up in mining. A circular was issued demanding that magistrates and officials desist in this speculation, or resign.

Magistrate Elwyn owned a share in a claim at Williams Creek, and when he read in the *British Colonist* of October 21, 1861, that a circular was about to be issued, he wrote to the secretary of the colony, advising him of his claim and stating that he had acquired it before the circular was written, but that he was prepared to resign if the governor so desired.

Elwyn pointed out to the government that over 120 mining disputes had been settled in his court during the mining season, only two of which had been appealed, and in each case his decision had been upheld by Chief Justice Matthew Baillie Begbie. However, as he would not give up his mining claim he was replaced by an Irish lawyer who had been judge of the small debts court for Hope and Yale. Andrew Charles Elliott was the second magistrate in Lillooet. He went on to high political offices, ending his career as Premier of British Columbia.

born in Ireland in 1829, he studied law under Joseph Chitty, the renowned lawyer and writer of legal books, and was admitted to the bar at Lincoln's Inn in 1854. Perhaps surprisingly for a competent legal man, Elliott was also adventurous. Hearing about the gold discoveries in British Columbia, he set out for the Colony of New Caledonia, arriving in Victoria in the summer of 1859 with his English wife Mary and four-year-old daughter Mary Rachel.

The Victoria *Gazette*, 8 October 1859, reported: "Andrew C. Elliott, Barrister at law, has been appointed a judge of the small debts court for Yale and Hope." The following correspondence from the Colonial Secretary's office, His Excellency Governor Seymour's files, stated the appointment:

A.C. Elliott

Sir,
    With reference to a conversation held between his excellency the Governor and yourself at Yale in September 1st, on the subject of your appointment as a County Court Judge in British Columbia, I now have the honor to enclose to you herewith your commission under the hand and seal of His Excellency to act as judge of such court.

2. Your jurisdiction will for the present be confined to the districts of Hope and Yale, and your salary will be at the rate of two hundred pounds per annum, to be increased when the fees of your court shall by their increase justify such a change.
3. You will be permitted to practise at the Assizes, provided always that such practice does not interfere with the business of the County Court.
4. Your court will have to be self-supporting, and all fees will have to be paid into the Public Treasury of the Colony.

    I have, etc.
    (sd) William A.G. Young
    Act. Col. Sec.

After a year in this post, Elliott was appointed Assistant Gold Commissioner and Stipendiary Magistrate at Lillooet in June 1861. This was a lonely time for Mary Elliott, who was the only white woman resident in the town. She especially enjoyed putting up Mrs. Martley while the Captain built his ranch home on Pavilion mountain. Fortunately, the large numbers of people continually passing through Lillooet kept the family busy and informed.

Andrew Elliott held many government posts; in 1865 he served in the Legislative Council of the Mainland Colony, then came back to Lillooet as magistrate and assistant gold commissioner. In 1867, after the union of the two colonies on March 18, he was appointed high sheriff of British Columbia, relinquishing his position as magistrate.

While he was assistant gold commissioner, Elliot, who was already astute in the ways of this new and practically undisciplined province, set about discovering the potential of virgin areas for gold and other natural resources. He sent capable men into the field and one of them, Andrew T. Jameson, gave an account of finding gold in the Bridge River area. His report of 9 October 1865 stated that he had been sent "to prospect for gold in that section of the country lying between the Chilcotin and Bridge Rivers and succeeded in finding gold in paying quantities at the headwaters of the latter stream."

After confederation, on 10 July 1871, Elliott became police magistrate for the city of Victoria, remaining in that position until he became a member of the legislative assembly in January 1876.

A few weeks after the sitting of the legislature in 1876, the Walken government resigned, and Andrew Charles Elliott became the fourth premier of British Columbia, as well as attorney general and provincial secretary. One of the first measures of his government was the repeal of the obnoxious Qualification and Registration of Voters Act, 1878. The Elliott government substituted for the cumbersome and unfair qualifications the plain requirement that a voter must be an adult male British subject who had resided in the province for twelve months and in the electoral district for two months before applying to be registered.

For two years Elliott piloted the provincial government, only to be defeated by the Walkem party when he himself lost his seat in May 1878. To the studious man of retiring nature, his defeat was a blow, and he retired from politics to spend his time in extensive travel. His daughter, Mary Rachel, married James William Douglas, son of Governor and Mrs. James Douglas, on 15 May 1878.

His last public duty was in 1884 at the Indian village of Metlakahtla, when he was one of the three commissioners appointed to look into the disturbances and discontent of the Indian people there.

Although he died in San Francisco, he was buried at his request in Victoria's Ross Cemetery beside his wife, and the Victoria *Colonist* gave a fitting epitaph to this gentle, studious man:

> He administered justice with a fearless hand and soon had discordant elements well in check. He was a genial, whole-souled gentleman of generous impulses and possessed the highest kind of honor. He was brave to a fault.

CHAPTER
9

"Ma" Murray in the 1930s

Lillooet's fortunes have been hitched to gold mining and recently, to sawmilling. Over the years many people have moved away, but always there have been others coming in to replace them. Of those who left, many are coming back to enjoy their retirement in the desertlike climate.

Where there were once large farms there are now subdivisions with modern houses and kitchen gardens. The Arts and Crafts Club encourages the new and the fine Lillooet Museum preserves the old, just as old-timers and newcomers meld into a true community. A group of promising artists living in Lillooet are beginning to be known around the province.

Among the visitors who come regularly to the town are rockhounds and lapidarians; they come often from great distances for Fraser River jade.

The local newspaper, the *Bridge River-Lillooet News*, was for many years read in the eastern provinces because of its famous early publisher, Mrs. Margaret Lally (Ma) Murray. She was known for her forthright and pithy editorials, and the town has often been referred to as "Ma Murray country."

Sawmilling and logging are the main industries of Lillooet today, but the British Columbia Railway—still called the PGE by residents along the line— is ever present. The sound of the Budd cars rolling smoothly northward, or of the freights shunting in the yards to add engines for the pull over Pavilion Mountain, are familiar sounds to all.

Now there are plans for a road from the coast which will again put Lillooet on the maps as a crossroads community.

Renee Chipman collection

A July 1 celebration in old Lillooet

INDEX